crochet
BASKETS

. . . .

36 Fun, Funky & Colorful Projects for Every Room in the House

Nola A. Heidbreder
Linda Pietz

SPRING HOUSE PRESS

DEDICATION
Soli Deo Gloria

THANKS
Many thanks to the dedicated crocheters who helped us by crocheting
the beautiful baskets!
Debbie Decker: Bathing Beauty Basket, Feather Basket, Flag Basket,
    Topsy-Turvy Tool Tote Basket
Bradley Duck: Rock 'n' Roll
Priscilla Pietz: 1970s Shag
Melissa Polumbus: Basket Weave Basket, Bridal Basket, Heart Basket

Front cover: Color Theory Nesting Baskets, page 123.
Back cover: Hook, Yarn, Crochet, page 57.

Publisher: Paul McGahren
Editorial Director: Matthew Teague
Editor: Kerri Grzybicki
Technical Editor: Charles Voth
Cover Design: Lindsay Hess
Interior Design: Ashley Millhouse
Layout: Michael Douglas
Illustration: Carolyn Mosher
Photography: Danielle Atkins

Spring House Press
3613 Brush Hill Court
Nashville, TN 37216
ISBN: 978-1-940611-61-7

Library of Congress Control Number: 2017930205
Printed in the USA
First Printing: March 2017

Note: The following list contains names used in *Crochet Baskets*
that may be registered with the United States Copyright Office: Beacon Adhesives
(Fabri-Tac); Bee Line Art Tools; Bernoulli Brew Werks; Berroco Inc. (Vintage); Bond
America; Brown Sheep Company, Inc. (Wildfoote Luxury Sock yarn); Bucilla; Caron;
Cascade (220); Cat's Cradle; Chunky Monkey; Clover Needlecraft, Inc. (Jumbo Tapestry
Needle, Wonder Clip); Coats and Clark; Craft Yarn Council; Denise Interchangeable
Knitting and Crochet; Derek Key; Dewberry Ridge; Dimensions; DMC (Pearl Cotton);
Dorr Mill Store; Dr. Seuss; Embellish-Knit!; Falk Fabrics LLC; Flickr; Frabjous Fibers;
Friedensreich Hundertwasser; Friedrich Stowasser; John Masefield; Lacis; Let Nola Do It,
LLC; Lion Brand Yarns; Lolo and Eddie; *Mary Engelbreit's Home Companion;* Minick and
Simpson; Paramount Wire (ParaWire); PattieWack Designs; Pepperell Braiding Company
(Bonnie Braid); Red Heart (Aunt Lydia's, Super Saver); *Rug Hooking Magazine;* Scünci;
Skif International; Tulle Source; Wool Novelty Company; Yummy Yarns (Jelly Yarn).

Photograph used on Picture This, page 51, taken by Derek Key and used under
the Creative Commons 2.0 license (https://creativecommons.org/licenses/by/2.0/).
View original image at www.flickr.com/photos/derekskey/sets/72157629697468872/
with/7184117186/. The image was modified to be black and white.

To learn more about Spring House Press books, or to find a retailer near you,
email info@springhousepress.com or visit us at www.springhousepress.com.

From back to front: "Dyed" Plarn, page 17; Spring Trio, page 79; Rock 'n' Roll, page 15.

contents

6 | Crochet Stitches and Techniques

15

Rock 'n' Roll

17

"Dyed" Plarn

33

Sunflower and
Daisy Variation

35

Bottle Cap Basket

39

Tulip Time

43

Topsy-Turvy Tool
Tote Basket

57

Hook, Yarn, Crochet

61

Loopy Pet Bed

63

Bird's Nest

67

Flower Garden

83

Scrappy Therapy

85

Feather Basket

89

Key to My Heart

91

Loopy Color Block Basket

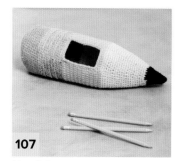

107

No. 2 Pencil

111

Polka Dot Dilemma

113

Roswell

117

Crown Jewels Basket

21 Flag Basket

23 A Penny for Your Thoughts

27 Woven

29 Blushing Beaded Alligator

45 Tiny Wire Basket

47 1970s Shag

51 Picture This

53 Hundertwasser's Spiral

69 Basket Weave Basket

73 Put a Lid on It!

75 Easter Parade

79 Spring Trio

95 Wave Your Flag

97 Bathing Beauty Basket

101 Bridal Basket

105 Heart Basket

119 Secret Saturated Sock Yarn

123 Color Theory Nesting Baskets

125 | Resources

127 | Index

Whether you are a pro at crocheting or completely new to the hobby, this section provides the basic stitches and techniques you need to know to succeed.

CROCHET STITCHES

Slipknot

1: Make a loop with the yarn, leaving a 6-inch tail, and pinch where it crosses itself. Lay this over the strand of yarn that leads to the ball of yarn (called the "working" yarn).

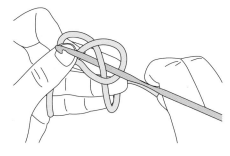

2: Insert the hook into the loop and under the strand of working yarn and lift it up through the loop. Gently pull on the tail to close the loop around the working yarn, which now forms the loop on the hook. This is called the "live" loop because if it comes off the hook, your crochet fabric will unravel.

Yarn Over (YO)

Right-hand crocheters: Wrap the yarn over your hook from back to front; some will prefer to rotate the hook counter-clockwise to make the wrap.

Left-hand crocheters: Wrap the yarn over your hook from back to front; some will prefer to rotate the hook clockwise to make the wrap.

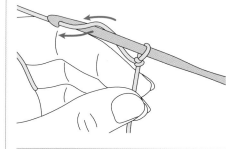

Chain (ch)

1: Make a slipknot on the hook.

2: Yarn over (YO) and pull the yarn through the loop on the hook. You will now have a loop on your hook, a chain stitch below the hook, and the slipknot below that first chain. Be sure the chains are loose enough that you can see a small space (about ⅓ of the width of the hook you are using) between the middle of a chain and the base of the next one.

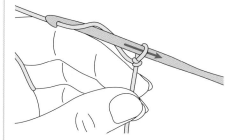

3: Repeat step 2 until you've crocheted the number of chains that were indicated in the pattern instructions. To count the chains, do not count the live loop nor the knot. Each V-shaped stitch between those two points is counted as a chain.

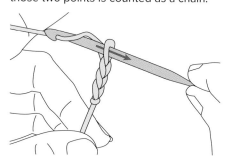

Slip Stitch (sl st)

Keep your tension comfortably loose to make this stitch. Insert the hook into the indicated stitch or space, yarn over, draw the strand of yarn through the insertion location and immediately through the loop on the hook.

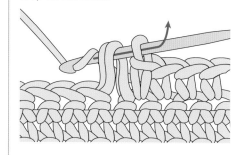

Single Crochet (sc)

1: Insert the hook into the indicated stitch, chain, or space and yarn over. Pull up the loop through the insertion point, giving you 2 loops on the hook.

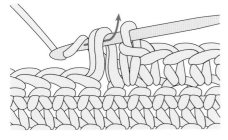

2: Yarn over and pull the strand through both loops on the hook to finish the single crochet.

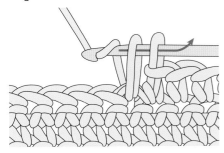

Half Double Crochet (hdc)

1: Wrap the yarn over the hook and insert the hook into the indicated stitch, chain, or space and yarn over again. Pull up the loop through the insertion point, giving you 3 loops on the hook.

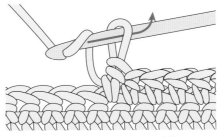

2: Yarn over and pull the strand through all 3 loops on the hook to finish the half double crochet.

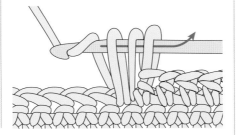

Double Crochet (dc)

1: Wrap the yarn over the hook and insert the hook into the indicated stitch, chain, or space and yarn over again. Pull up the loop through the insertion point, giving you 3 loops on the hook.

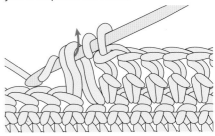

2: Yarn over and pull the strand through the first two loops on the hook.

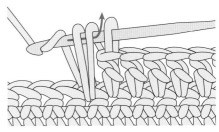

3: Repeat step 2 to finish the double crochet stitch.

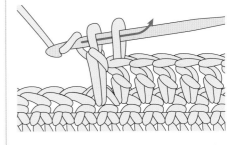

Treble Crochet (tr)

1: Wrap the yarn over the hook twice and insert the hook into the indicated stitch, chain, or space and yarn over again. Pull up the loop through the insertion point, giving you 4 loops on the hook.

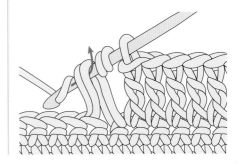

Loopy Color Block Basket, page 91.

2: Yarn over and pull the strand through the first 2 loops on the hook.

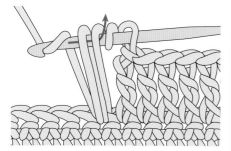

3: Repeat step 2.

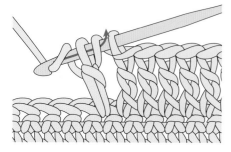

4: Repeat step 2 to finish the treble crochet stitch.

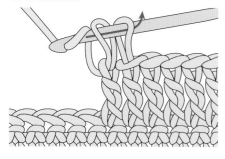

Post Stitches

Post stitches can cause stitches from previous rows to stand out towards the facing side of the fabric (called front posts) or to recede into the background (called back posts). Single, half double, double, and treble crochet stitches can all be made as post stitches. A post stitch is worked around the next indicated stitch by inserting the hook in and out of the fabric such that the post (or lower part) of the stitch worked around either recedes into the fabric or pushes out toward the crocheter.

For back post stitches (receding), insert the hook from the back of the fabric to the front in the gap before the post of the indicated stitch. Then, from the front, push the hook back through the fabric to the back in the gap after the indicated stitch. Yarn over and then pull back the strand through both sides of the indicated stitch and up to allow the rest of the stitch to be made.

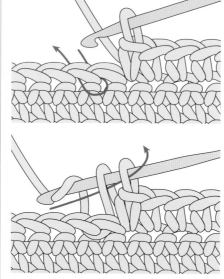

For front post stitches, insert the hook from the front to the back and then to the front again, beginning in the gap before the post of the indicated stitch around to the gap after the same post. Yarn over and complete the rest of the stitch.

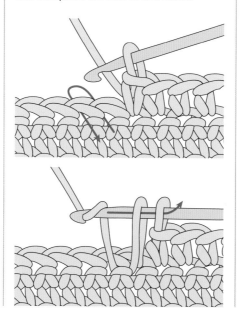

Skipping Stitches (sk)

As the pattern indicates, count the number of stitches and then proceed to work the next stitches in the next insertion point given in the instructions.

Two Single Crochet Decreases (sc2tog)

Version A

1: Insert hook in next stitch, yarn over, and pull up a loop.

2: Repeat step 1 in next stitch.

3: Yarn over and pull through all 3 loops on hook.

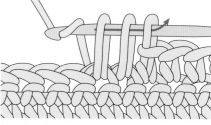

Version B

Some yarns leave more gaps than others, so this is an alternative to avoid gaps.

1: Insert hook in front loop only of next stitch.

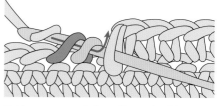

2: Repeat step 1 in next stitch.

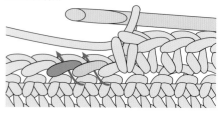

3: Yarn over and draw through all loops on hook.

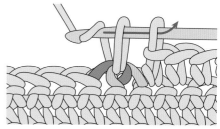

Bridal Basket, page 91.

Secret Saturated Sock Yarn, page 119.

CROCHET TECHNIQUES

Where to Work Stitches

Each chain stitch has two strands that look like a braid or hearts. When the chain is held horizontally with the right side up, the strand closest to you is called the front loop and the strand facing away from you is the back loop. When working into a starting chain to work in back and forth rows, it is possible to insert the hook in one of the following three places. Choose the one you like best and stay consistent across the first row of stitches.

First, insert the hook under just the back loop and finish the stitch as instructed.

Second, insert the hook under the back loop together with the strand of yarn that is under it.

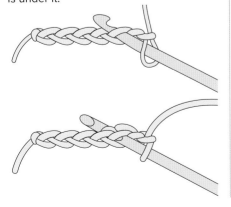

Third, flip the chain over to reveal a ridge on the back of each chain stitch. Insert the hook under each ridge to make a stitch. This is called working into the back bump, ridge, or bar.

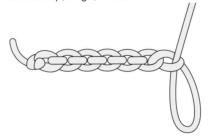

Once you are working into other stitches and not into chains, the hook should be inserted under both loops at the top of the stitches from the previous row. Only insert the hook differently if told to. Instructions may say to make a single crochet in the back loop only, in which case find the strand furthest from you and insert the hook under it. If the instructions say to insert the hook

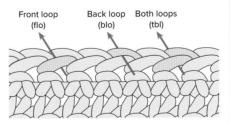

in the front loop only, insert the hook under the top strand that is closest to you. When you aren't supposed to work the top two usual strands for the whole

row, instructions will be given at the beginning of the row or round explaining what to do for the entire row or round.

In some instances, stitches are skipped and replaced with a chain or a series of chain stitches that strand across the missed stitch(es), making a gap called a chain space. Unless indicated otherwise, on following rows or rounds, it is usual to insert the hook completely under the chain strand into that gap or "chain space" (ch-sp) and to finish the stitch you are making from that point.

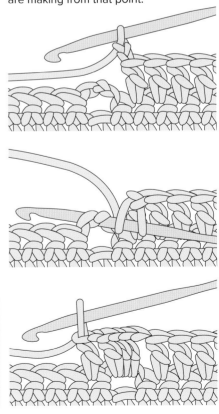

Working in Rows

Many patterns involve working across a row, then turning and continuing with the following row. Some instructions will ask you to make some chain stitches to bring the hook up to the same height of the stitches you are about to make across the new row; this is called a "turning chain" (tch).

In some cases, a turning chain will stand in for another stitch. This will be indicated as follows: Ch 3 (counts as first double crochet). In this case, the stitch at the base of the turning chain will be skipped and the next stitch should be considered the second stitch of the row. When working back on the following row, the turning chain that counts as a double crochet will be the last stitch to be worked into and you should be careful to crochet into that turning chain to get the correct number of stitches for that row. All exceptions should be stated in the pattern.

In some cases, turning chains will not count as the first stitch and will read as follows: "Ch 1, sc in first 2 sts." The initial ch 1 is the turning chain, but it is not counted as a stitch. When you work back toward the end of the following row, you would not crochet into that ch 1 in order to get the right stitch count.

Working in the Round

Some patterns are worked in a joined round. Work a slip stitch into the top of the first stitch of the round as instructed. You may or may not be asked to turn the work to go in the opposite direction. Some patterns are worked in a spiral round without a slip stitch join. At the end of the round, keep crocheting into the next round. Use a stitch marker to mark the beginning of the round.

Working into Both Sides of a Starting Chain

1: To crochet along both sides of a starting chain, start by inserting the hook under the back ridge loops of the chain and then rotate the work with the same side facing rather than turning to work back along the stitches just made.

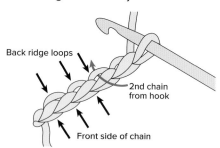

Back ridge loops

2nd chain from hook

Front side of chain

Topsy-Turvy Tool Tote Basket, page 43.

2: Crochet the indicated number of chain stitches given in the pattern instructions. Work the first stitch into the back ridge of the 2nd stitch from the hook. To find this first stitch easily, place a stitch marker in it. Crochet the remaining stitches as indicated to the end of the starting chain. In the last stitch next to the slip knot, there will usually be more than one stitch worked; follow the pattern. Rotate the piece 180 degrees to continue into the other side of the starting chain.

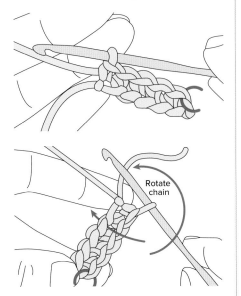

3: Insert the hook under both strands at the top of each chain as you work across this side. When you reach the last stitch, the instructions will most likely have you increase there with more than one stitch. Then you will join to the first stitch (the one with the marker) with a slip stitch or continue in a spiral fashion without joins.

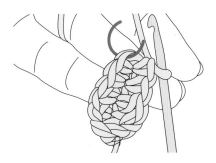

Adjustable Ring (AR)

This reduces the size of the hole in your starting round.

1: Make a ring with the yarn that has a 6-inch tail. As you would for a slip knot, put the hook in the loop.

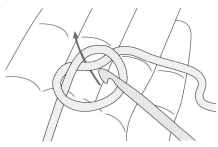

2: Yarn over the hook. Pull the yarn through the loop for a slip stitch, but don't tighten it.

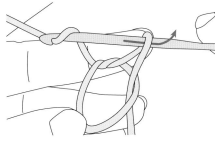

3: Chain 1 and, over both strands of yarn that make the adjustable ring, proceed to single crochet the number of times instructed. Pull the tail to close the ring.

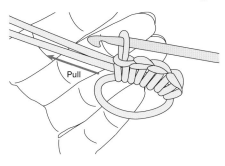

Make the next stitch of the next round in the first single crochet of the finished ring.

Right Side (RS) and Wrong Side (WS)

The side of the work that will eventually be the "public" side is called the right side of the work. Pattern instructions that involve rows or rounds being worked in both directions with turns and turning chains will indicate which rows or rounds are the right side of the work. It is not always the odd rows that are the right side of the work. The front loops and back loops of the top of the chain are relative to the person crocheting, not relative to the right or the wrong side of the work. When you are crocheting with the right side facing you, the front loops of the stitches are the ones nearest you, but if you turn the work, those loops now become the back loops of the stitches because they are furthest from you.

Changing Colors

To change colors, or to add a new ball of yarn in the same color, crochet to the place just before you make the last stitch with the current color. In the next stitch, make the indicated stitch to the point where there are 2 loops left on the hook (3 loops for half double crochet). Let go of (called "dropping") the strand of the current color; leaving a tail, yarn over with the new color and pull it through the last 2 loops on the hook. Gently tighten the loops with both tails and proceed to crochet following stitches with the new color. The tails, or "ends," will be hidden in the crochet fabric, or "woven in" after more of the fabric has been crocheted.

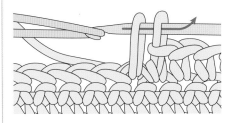

Knots in the Yarn

Do not crochet a knot into the fabric. Stop crocheting when there are 6 inches before the knot and cut as close as possible to both sides of the knot. Continue to join the yarn into the next stitch as if you were changing colors.

Invisible Fasten Off

1: Cut yarn, leaving a 4-inch tail, and pull end out of top of last stitch without tugging too hard.

2: Thread tail in tapestry needle; from wrong side to right side, insert needle under the two top loops of the 2nd stitch of the round.

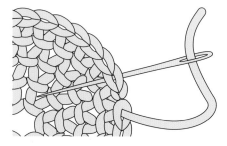

3: Pull until the stitch looks the same size as neighboring stitches. Insert the tapestry needle into the heart of the stitch from which the tail exits.

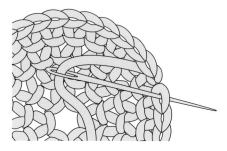

4: Pull the tail through to the wrong side of the work. Weave in the end under back strands of various stitches to secure tail before trimming close.

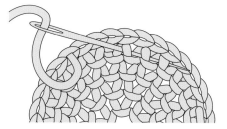

Puff Stitch

A puff stitch is a combination of half double crochet stitches that are all worked as a group into one insertion point. Puff stitches can be built out of 3, 4, or 5 stitches. The pattern will specify this number. Yarn over, insert hook in indicated stitch or space the number of times indicated, yarn over, and pull through all loops on hook. The illustration shows a 3-hdc puff stitch.

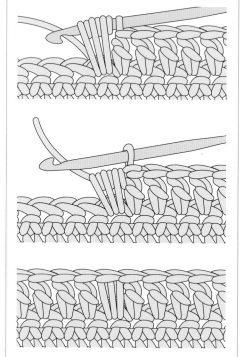

Clusters

Clusters come in two forms: bobble clusters and decreasing clusters. Bobble clusters are often simply called clusters and are worked into one insertion point. They typically are made of double crochet stitches, but it is possible to make them from treble crochet stitches or double-treble stitches. The pattern will define which stitches and how many to use. To make a bobble cluster with double crochet stitches:

1: Yarn over. Insert hook in indicated stitch. Yarn over. Pull up loop, yarn over, and pull through 2 loops on hook.

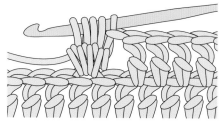

2: Repeat step 1 the number of times indicated (usually 3, but 2, 4, or more is also possible).

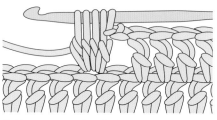

3: Yarn over and pull through all loops on the hook. The illustration shows a 4-dc bobble cluster (4dc-cl).

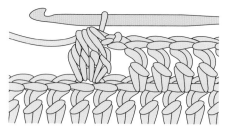

Decreasing clusters are worked in a similar way, but are worked into a series of insertion points usually, but not always, immediately next to each other. Decreasing clusters are labeled with the number used, the stitch used, and the word "together." In the illustration, you can see a dc4tog (double crochet 4 together). When this stitch is made, the hook goes into 4 different insertion points to make the bottom part of a double crochet. 4 stitches become 1 stitch, which is a decrease of 3 stitches. In some patterns, other chains or stitches are used to replace the missing 3 stitches, so the total number of stitches on a row or round does not decrease. Decreasing clusters are used both to create inverted triangle shapes and to actually decrease stitches; the pattern will explain the specifics for each situation.

1: To make a dc4tog, yarn over, insert hook in NEXT indicated stitch, and yarn over. Pull up loop, yarn over, pull through 2 loops on hook.

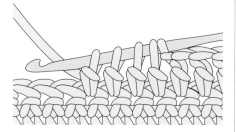

2: Repeat step 1 4 times; yarn over, and pull through all 5 loops on hook.

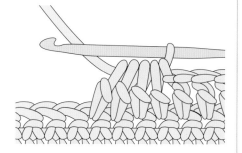

FINISHING STITCHES

Whip Stitch

This technique of sewing flat seams is one of the fastest. Line up the sides of the two pieces with their right sides together. With a tapestry needle and yarn, insert the needle from back to front through both layers of crocheted fabric and pull out on the side facing you. A short length further along the sides, re-insert the needle from the back through to the front of both layers and repeat across. Pull evenly and keep stitches tight as you work across. Normally, if you are working along sides that have the tops of the stitches visible, you can either work under all four strands of each pair of stitches, first under the two strands of the stitch on the back piece and then under the strands of the corresponding stitch on the front piece. This creates a small ridge on the inside of the seam. To lessen this ridge, insert the needle under the front loop only of the stitch on the rear piece of crocheted fabric and then under the back loop only of the corresponding stitch on the front piece of crochet.

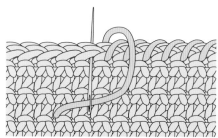

Mattress Stitch

This seaming technique produces a tight and almost invisible ridge that is very secure. Lay the two crocheted pieces to be seamed with right side up and their edges matching each other. Along the edges that you are joining, find an insertion point (A) and an exit point (B) on the piece that is closest to you. Insert the tapestry needle threaded with yarn into A and out of B. Look for the corresponding segment of fabric—it may be a stitch, row, or section of a row on the opposite piece of crochet—and insert the needle into C and exit from D. The insertion point (C) and the exit point (D) are usually off-center from the corresponding points on the first piece of fabric rather than directly lined up with each other (see illustration).

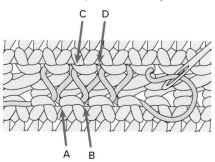

Color Theory Nesting Baskets, page 123.

Scrappy Therapy, page 83.

Rock 'n' Roll

FINISHED MEASUREMENTS: 7-in. wide by 4-in. high   **GAUGE:** 3 sc = 1 inch

A guitar pick punch is a tool that allows you to punch out guitar picks—just like it sounds. Being musically challenged, I thought it a nice idea for guitar players, but what could I possibly do with such a device? That was my feeling until I visited the gift shop of our local art museum and fell in love with a necklace made from guitar picks punched from credit and gift cards. It was then that the light bulb came on. Like me, you can be musically challenged and still enjoy crocheting this basket while listening to some vintage rock 'n' roll.

YARN

MATERIALS & TOOLS

- 1 skein Red Heart Super Saver yarn in 3933 Dove (5 oz/236 yds)
- H hook
- 24 guitar picks
- Drill and small drill bit
- 8mm split jump rings
- 8mm jump rings
- Small pliers
- Stitch marker
- Optional: Guitar pick punch

Crocheted by Bradley Duck

Guitar Picks

Drill a small hole into the top of the guitar picks. Insert guitar pick and the split jump ring into each regular jump ring. Close regular jump ring.

Bottom

Make a slip knot, ch 4, and join into ring with a sl st.

Rnd 1: 6 sc into ring. Place sm on the last st—remove each rnd and place on the new last st.

Rnd 2: 2 sc in each sc. (12 sc)

Rnd 3: *Sc in next sc, 1 sc in next sc. Repeat from * across the rnd. (18 sc)

Rnd 4: *2 sc in next sc, sc in each of next 2 sc. Repeat from * across the rnd. (24 sc)

Rnd 5: *2 sc in next sc, sc in each of next 3 sc. Repeat from * across the rnd. (30 sc)

Rnd 6: *2 sc in next sc, sc in each of next 4 sc. Repeat from * across the rnd. (36 sc)

Rnd 7: *2 sc in next sc, sc in each of next 5 sc. Repeat from * across the rnd. (42 sc)

Rnd 8: *2 sc in next sc, sc in each of next 6 sc. Repeat from * across the rnd. (48 sc)

Rnd 9: *2 sc in next sc, sc in each of next 7 sc. Repeat from * across the rnd. (54 sc)

Rnd 10: *2 sc in next sc, sc in each of next 8 sc. Repeat from * across the rnd. (60 sc)

Rnd 11: *2 sc in next sc, sc in each of next 9 sc. Repeat from * across the rnd. (66 sc)

Rnd 12: *2 sc in next sc, sc in each of next 10 sc in back loop only. Repeat from * across the rnd. (72 sc)

Sides

Crochet 10 rows without increasing for the basket sides.

Next rnd: *2 sc in next 2 sc, insert hook into jump ring, then into the next sc. Make sure that the side of the guitar pick you want to show is facing out. Complete the sc.* Repeat between the * for a total of 24 times. Sc 1 rnd ending with a sl st. Break yarn and work in ends.

"dyed" plarn

FINISHED MEASUREMENTS: 6½-in. wide by 11½-in. high   **GAUGE:** 1½ sc = 1 inch

I once attended a workshop on using recycled materials for art. One of the revolutionary techniques I learned was to apply acrylic paint to the numerous plastic grocery bags each of us collects, and then cut them into strips. The resulting product is called "plarn," for "plastic yarn." I was immediately inspired to create a crocheted basket with this fantastic recycled material.

Note that spray paint does not work well on plarn—as you crochet, spray paint tends to flake off the plastic surface. It is also important to crochet a strand of yarn with the plarn to give it strength.

MATERIALS & TOOLS

- 1 skein Red Heart Super Saver yarn 0376 Burgundy (7 oz/364 yds)
- 50 white plastic grocery bags
- N hook
- Newspaper
- Stitch marker
- Sea sponge
- Paint brush
- Acrylic paints in yellow, orange, red, red-violet, and violet

Note: Hold one strand each of plarn and yarn throughout.

Prepare the Plarn

1: Lay plastic bags out flat on newspaper.

2: Slightly dilute your acrylic paint (enough so it flows easily).

3: Brush, sponge, and splatter paint onto the bags. The bags were only painted on one side for the sample, but both sides can be painted if you don't want any white showing.

4: Let the paint dry.

5: With the bags flat, cut off the very bottom. Cut every 2 inches to create loops.

6: To join, put one loop inside another. Insert the end of that loop back through itself and pull gently to snug. Continue to join loops and roll into a ball.

Bottom

Make a slip knot, ch 4, and join into ring with a sl st.

Rnd 1: 6 sc into ring. Place sm on the last st. Remove each rnd and place on the new last st.

Rnd 2: 2 sc in each sc. (12 sc)

Rnd 3: *2 sc in next sc, 1 sc in next sc. Repeat from * across the rnd. (18 sc)

Rnd 4: *2 sc in next sc, sc in each of next 2 sc. Repeat from * across the rnd. (24 sc)

Rnd 5: *2 sc in next sc, sc in each of next 3 sc. Repeat from * across the rnd. (30 sc)

Rnd 6: *2 sc in next sc, sc in each of next 4 sc. Repeat from * across the rnd. (36 sc)

Rnd 7: *2 sc in next sc, sc in each of next 5 sc. Repeat from * across the rnd. (42 sc)

Rnd 8: *2 sc in next sc, sc in each of next 6 sc. Repeat from * across the rnd. (48 sc)

Rnd 9: *2 sc in next sc, sc in each of next 7 sc. Repeat from * across the rnd. (54 sc)

Side

Continue to sc without increases until the side measures 4½ inches. On the next rnd, ch 9, sc 18, ch 9, sc 18. Sc 2 more rnds, making sure to sc into the ch sts of the previous rnd. This will create handles. Work in ends.

flag basket

FINISHED MEASUREMENTS: 13-in. wide by 5-in. deep by 4½-in. high   **GAUGE:** 2 dc = 1¼ inch

Hip hip hooray for the red, white, and blue! Let's show off our love of our great country, and our love for crocheting with this basket. This works up quickly to make a nice, sturdy, patriotic basket. It's the perfect size for a loaf of bread or a bottle of wine.

MATERIALS & TOOLS

- 24 x 72-in. off-white cotton fabric, washed and dried (color A)
- 12 x 72-in. red cotton fabric, washed and dried (color B)
- 4 yds blue cotton fabric, washed and dried (color C)
- P hook
- Scissors or rotary cutter
- Sewing thread to match fabric
- Sewing needle
- Jumbo tapestry needle (such as Clover)

Crocheted by Debbie Decker

Prepare the Fabrics

1: You will be snipping and ripping (or using a rotary cutter) to transform your cotton fabrics into strips. The off-white and red fabrics should be made into 2 x 72-inch strips, and the blue fabric into 2-inch x 4-yard strips.

2: Join strips as necessary by folding the edge of the strip over about 1 inch. Cut a ½-inch slit into the folded edge of the strip. Repeat with the strip you want to join. Lay the slits on top of each other, with tails facing in opposite directions. Take the tail that is on top and pull it through the bottom of the slits. Pull the two tails in opposite directions. This will tighten the joining knot. Repeat as necessary.

Bottom

Row 1: Starting with color A, ch 18. Dc in third ch from hook. 1 dc in each of next 15 chains. YO and insert hook into last ch. YO and pull up loop. With 2 loops of color A on hook, YO with color B and pull through 2 loops on hook. The new color is now added. (16 dc) Ch 2 and turn.

Row 2: Dc in next 15 dc. YO and insert hook into ch 2 sp. YO and pull up loop. YO with color A and pull through 2 loops on hook. The new color is now added. (16 dc) Ch 2 and turn.

Row 3: Dc in next 15 dc and ch 2 sp. (16 dc) End.

Sides

Row 1: With color C, ch 18. Dc in third ch from hook. 1 dc in each of next 16 chains. (17 dc) Ch 2 and turn.

Row 2: Dc in each dc across and in ch 2 sp. (17 dc) Ch 2 and turn.

Row 3: Dc in each dc across and in ch 2 sp. (17 dc) End.

Repeat Rows 1–3 for the other side.

Ends

Row 1: Ch 7. Dc in third ch from hook and 6 across. (6 dc) Ch 2 and turn.

Row 2: Dc. In each dc across and in ch 2 sp. (6 dc) Ch 2 and turn.

Row 3: Dc in each dc across and in ch 2 sp. (6 dc) End.

Repeat Rows 1–3 for the other end.

Finish

Pin sides and ends to bottom and hand-sew together with matching thread.

a penny for your thoughts

It was with great excitement during my college days that I discovered a beautiful blue fabric embroidered with tiny mirrors. This was my first introduction to shisha embroidery. Mirrored embroidery originated in ancient India. At first, small pieces of mica were used, but coins and even silver were also used in place of the mica. As time went on, embroiderers favored silvered glass mirrors. In the ancient tradition of this art, I used pennies instead of mirrors. One small benefit to creating this basket is that if you're short a penny, you'll always know where seven of them are.

YARN

MEDIUM

MATERIALS & TOOLS

- 1 skein Cascade 220 in 2429 Ireland (3½ oz/220 yds)
- 1 skein Cascade 220 in 2445 Shire (3½ oz/220 yds)
- G hook
- DMC Pearl Cotton embroidery thread in 4025 (Size 5)
- 7 pennies
- Sewing needle
- White glue
- Stitch marker

Note: Hold one strand from each color throughout.

Crochet the Basket

Make a slip knot. Ch 2.

Rnd 1: Sc 6 into second ch from hook. Place sm on the last sc in the rnd. Replace into last stitch every rnd.

Rnd 2: Sc 2 in each of 6 sc around. (12 sc)

Rnd 3: *Sc 2 in next sc, 1 sc in next sc. Repeat from * across the rnd. (18 sc)

Rnd 4: *Sc 2 in next sc, 1 sc in each of next 2 sc. Repeat from * across the rnd. (24 sc)

Rnd 5: *Sc 2 in next sc, 1 sc in each of next 3 sc. Repeat from * across the rnd. (30 sc)

Rnd 6: *Sc 2 in next sc, 1 sc in each of next 4 sc. Repeat from * across the rnd. (36 sc)

Rnd 7: *Sc 2 in next sc, 1 sc in each of next 5 sc. Repeat from * across the rnd. (42 sc)

Rnd 8: *Sc 2 in next sc, 1 sc in each of next 6 sc. Repeat from * across the rnd. (48 sc)

Rnd 9: *Sc 2 in next sc, 1 sc in each of next 7 sc. Repeat from * across the rnd. (54 sc)

Rnd 10: Sc across the rnd.

Rnd 11: *Sc 2 in next sc, 1 sc in each of next 8 sc. Repeat from * across the rnd. (60 sc)

Rnds 12–18: Sc across the rnd.

Rnd 19: *Sl st 1, sc, hdc, dc, 2 tr, dc, hdc, sc, sl st 1. Repeat from * across the rnd. Sl st 1 into the beginning sl st 1 of the rnd. Break yarn and work in ends.

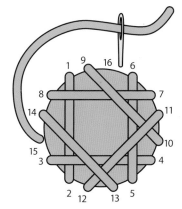

Sew down each penny by making the stitches as shown from 1 to 2, 3 to 4, etc.

Shisha Embroidery

1: Glue pennies below the high point of the wavy edge. There will be six pennies on the sides. Glue one at the center of the bottom of the basket. Allow glue to dry.

2: Using one yard of cotton embroidery thread per penny, follow the illustration below to embroider the pennies to the basket.

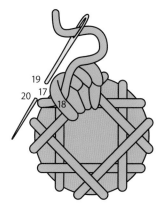

To make the decorative frame stitching, come up at 17 and insert the needle under the stitches from the center out. Draw the needle to the right side of the working thread at 18. Make a stitch from 18 to 19 and come up at 20. Repeat. This is a buttonhole stitch all the way around the penny.

woven

As a child, I remember being envious of the class across the hall that got to make baskets. They paraded out every afternoon to sit on the lawn outside our windows, weaving away. It was then that I became determined to unlock the mystery of basket weaving. Unfortunately, it was not until I became an adult that I realized my dream of learning this skill. Although willow, reed, and pine needles are the most common materials for weaving, I wondered if a stiff crocheted strip would work as a weaver. My experiment worked, and a crocheted edging on the top held everything together. Success!

Looking for slightly mindless project? This is perfect. After crocheting the strips, the basket weaves up very quickly.

YARN

Materials & Tools

- Berroco Vintage worsted yarn (3½ oz/218 yds) in the following colors:
  - 6 skeins 5176 Pumpkin (color A)
  - 3 skeins 5164 Tang (color B)
  - 1 skein 5134 Sour Cherry (color C)
- G hook
- Scrap yarn in a contrasting color

Note: Hold two strands together throughout.

Crochet the Strips

1: Using color A, ch 9. Sc in second chain from hook and across the row, ch 1, turn. (8 sc)

2: *Sc across the next row, making sure to maintain 8 sc. Ch 1, turn. Repeat from * until a total of 110 rows is completed. Break yarn and work in ends. Make 10 strips in color A.

3: Using color B, ch 9. Sc in second chain from hook and across the row, ch 1, turn. (8 sc)

4: *Sc across the next row, making sure to maintain 8 sc. Ch 1, turn. Repeat from * until a total of 200 rows is completed. Break yarn and work in ends. Make three strips in color B.

Weaving the Basket

1: Place five color A strips on a flat surface with wrong side facing up.

Weave the other five strips with wrong side facing up over/under as per the illustration below, making sure to center the strips. Pin together if desired.

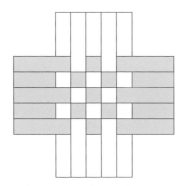

Weave the strips together as shown.

2: Starting in one corner and holding up the strips, sc around the top edge of the strips using scrap yarn. Ch 1 in between each strip, including the corners. This will make it easier to weave the sides.

3: Taking one color B strip at a time and starting in a corner, weave over/under around the basket. Join strip ends with a sl st. Push this down toward the bottom

of the basket. Next, weave the middle strip and finally the top strip; join strip ends with a sl st.

Top Edge

Rnd 1: Starting in the corner where you started the scrap yarn, sc. Using color C, sc around the top with 8 sc in the top of each strip and 1 ch in between each strip and at the corners. When reaching the beginning, join with sl st, ch 1. Remove the scrap yarn a little bit at a time while crocheting the color C edge.

Rnd 2: Sc around the top, once again joining the end with the beginning using sl st into the ch 1.

Rnd 3: Ch 1, crab stitch (reverse sc) around outer edge. Join beginning to end with a sl st in the ch 1. Break yarn and work in ends.

blushing beaded alligator

FINISHED MEASUREMENTS: 4½-in. wide by 2½-in. high; 6-in. wide by 3-in. high
GAUGE: 5 sc = 1 inch

Periodically, my sisters and I would be shipped off to relatives in Florida. This thrill-seeking side of the family enjoyed water skiing in an alligator-riddled lake. There was even a relative who wanted us to have an up-close-and-personal peek at an alligator—one was hidden in an enclosed porch and another in the bathroom tub. Despite these death-defying experiences, I do like alligators. I just don't want to swim with or otherwise socialize with them! This basket's texture reminds me of the interesting texture and pattern of alligator skin, and you won't have to worry about any snapping jaws when you create this interesting basket.

YARN

MATERIALS & TOOLS

- 2 skeins per basket Cascade 220 in 2449* (3½ oz/220 yds)
- E hook
- Size 8 beads in color of choice, 40 for smaller and 80 for larger basket
- Small sewing needle
- Strong thread, such as quilting thread
- Stitch marker

  *The yarn pictured is Cascade 220 in 9441, which has been discontinued.

Bead Strand

1: Thread a sewing needle with 4 inches of sewing thread, double it over, and tie a knot at the end.

2: Insert yarn end into the sewing thread loop.

3: Thread beads onto the sewing needle and slide them down onto the yarn. Hole sizes on the beads vary, so some beads may not slide onto the yarn. For the small basket, thread 40 beads; thread 80 for the larger basket. For each basket, there are few extra beads in case one should break. Slide beads down as you crochet the basket.

Bottom

Rnd 1: Make a slip knot. Ch 4, join into ring with a sl st. Sc 6 sts into the ring. Place a sm in the last st. Remove and place the sm in the last st of every rnd.

Rnd 2: Increase by crocheting two sts into every st. (12 sc)

Rnd 3: Sc in next st, 2 sc in next st. (18 sc)

Rnd 4: 2 sc in next st, sc in each of next 2 sts. (24 sc)

Rnd 5: Sc in each of next 3 sts, 2 sc in next st. (30 sc)

Rnd 6: 2 sc in next st, sc in each of next 4 sts. (36 sc)

Rnd 7: Sc in each of next 5 sts, 2 sc in next st. (42 sc)

Rnd 8: 2 sc in next st, sc in each of next 6 sts. (48 sc)

Rnd 9: Sc in each of next 7 sts, 2 sc in next st. (54 sc)

Rnd 10: 2 sc in next st, sc in each of next 8 sts. (60 sc)

Rnd 11: Sc in each of next 9 sts, 2 sc in next st. (66 sc)

Rnd 12: 2 sc in next st, sc in each of next 10 sts. (72 sc) Note: For smaller basket, end increases here and crochet 2 rnd sc. Do not break yarn.

Rnd 13: Sc in each of next 11 sts, 2 sc in next st. (78 sc)

Rnd 14: 2 sc in next st, sc in each of next 12 sts. (84 sc)

Rnd 15: Sc in each of next 13 sts, 2 sc in next st. (90 sc)

Rnd 16: 2 sc in next st, sc in each of next 14 sts. (96 sc)

Rnd 17: Sc in each of next 15 sts, 2 sc in next st. (102 sc) Note: For larger basket, end increases here and crochet 3 rnd sc. Do not break yarn.

Sides

Rnd 1: Ch 4, dc in same sc. Ch 1, skip 2 sc, dc in next sc, ch 1. *Skip 2 sc, 2 dc in next sc, ch 1, skip 2 sc, dc in next sc, ch 1. Repeat from * across the rnd. Join to top of beginning ch with a sl st. This creates the framework to attach the alligator scales.

Rnd 2: With right side of basket facing, YO, insert hook under first dc post and up between the 2 dc from the previous rnd. YO and complete first dc. Crochet 4 more dc around the dc post, sl st bead in place, and ch 1. Turn basket upside down with right side still facing, 5 dc around second post.

Turn basket right side up, sl st into top of dc from previous rnd. *Continue with 5 dc around first post, sl st bead, ch 1, 5 dc around second post, sl st into top of dc from previous rnd. Repeat from * across the rnd. The small basket will have 12 scales and the large basket 17.

Rnd 3: Ch 4, skip 2 sc, 2 dc in next sc, ch 1. *Skip 2 sc, dc in next sc, ch 1, skip 2 sc, 2 dc in next sc, ch 1. Repeat from * across the rnd. Sl st into top of beginning ch.

Rnd 4: Follow directions for crocheting alligator scales (rnd 2), starting with a scale around the first dc post cluster. End with a sl st in the top of last dc.

Rnds 5–6: Repeat rnds 1–2. For small basket, break yarn and work in ends. There will be 3 rnds of scales. For larger basket, repeat rnds 3–4 once more. Break yarn and work in ends. There will be 4 rnd of scales.

sunflower and daisy variation

SUNFLOWER FINISHED MEASUREMENTS: 4-in. wide by 2½-in. high and 6-in. wide by 2½-in. high
GAUGE: 5 sc = 1 inch

Growing up, our house was surrounded by greenhouses. My curiosity often found me wandering over to gaze at the brightly colored rows of flowers. To this day, the daisy and the sunflower never fail to put a smile on my face. May these bright baskets put a little grin on your face when you make them.

YARN

MEDIUM

MATERIALS & TOOLS

Sunflower
- 1 skein each Cascade 220 yarn (3½ oz/220 yds) in the following colors:
  - 9486 Shamrock (Color A)
  - 7827 Goldenrod (Color B)
  - 9445 Green and Orange Blend (Color C)
- E hook

Daisy Variation
- 1 skein each Cascade 220 yarn (3½ oz/220 yds) in the following colors:
  - 9486 Shamrock (Color A)
  - 8010 Natural (Color B)
  - 7827 Goldenrod (Color C)
- E hook

Small Sunflower

Using color A, follow directions for Blushing Beaded Alligator (page 29) through rnd 12, 2 rnd sc. Break yarn and join color B. Follow directions for basket sides. Crochet rnds 1 to 4. Break yarn and join color C.

Small Sunflower Center

Rnd 1: 3 sc in each ch 1 space from previous rnd. (72 sc) Join with sl st.

Rnd 2: Ch 1, sc in next 9 sc, dec 1. *Sc in next 10 sc, dec 1.* Repeat between the * across the rnd. Sl st in beginning ch 1.

Rnd 3: Ch 1, sc in next 8 sc, dec 1. *Sc in next 9 sc, dec 1.* Repeat between the * across the rnd. Sl st in beginning ch 1.

Rnd 4: Ch 1, sc in next 7 sc, dec 1. *Sc in next 8 sc, dec 1.* Repeat between the * across the rnd. Sl st in beginning ch 1. Break yarn and work in ends.

Large Sunflower

Using color A, follow directions for Blushing Beaded Alligator through rnd 17, 3 rnd sc. Break yarn and join color B. Follow directions for basket sides. Crochet rnds 1 to 4. Break yarn and join color C.

Large Sunflower Center

Rnd 1: 3 sc in each ch 1 space from previous rnd. (102 sc) Join with sl st.

Rnd 2: Ch 1, sc in next 14 sc, dec 1. *Sc in next 15 sc, dec 1.* Repeat between the * across the rnd. Sl st in beginning ch 1.

Rnd 3: Ch 1, sc in next 13 sc, dec 1. *Sc in next 14 sc, dec 1.* Repeat between the * across the rnd. Sl st in beginning ch 1.

Rnd 4: Ch 1, sc in next 12 sc, dec 1. *Sc in next 13 sc, dec 1.* Repeat between the * across the rnd. Sl st in beginning ch 1.

Rnd 5: Ch 1, sc in next 11 sc, dec 1. *Sc in next 12 sc, dec 1.* Repeat between the * across the rnd. Sl st in beginning ch 1. Break yarn and work in ends.

Daisy Variation

Using color A, follow directions for Blushing Beaded Alligator through rnd 12, 2 rnd sc. Break yarn and join color B. Follow directions for basket sides with the following changes:

Ch 5 in place of ch 4. Tr in place of dc. Crochet 7 dc around each post with a ch 1 between each side of the scale/petal. Complete rnds 1 to 4 of basket sides on the Blushing Beaded Alligator. Break yarn and join color C.

Follow directions for small sunflower center. Break yarn and work in ends.

bottle cap basket

FINISHED MEASUREMENTS: 7-in. wide by 4-in. high   **GAUGE:** 4 sc = 1 inch

Way back when, I found a necklace made with vintage grape soda bottle caps. It was a little pricey, but I never regretted purchasing it. Over the years, each time I have worn this piece, I have been showered with compliments. Since then, I have collected old bottle caps and made many necklaces. Bottle caps also make a great embellishment for a basket, and thus the Bottle Cap Basket was born. It's funny where creative inspiration pops up.

YARN

MEDIUM

MATERIALS & TOOLS

- 1 skein Berroco Vintage worsted in 5116 Dove (3½ oz/218 yds) (Color A)
- 1 skein Berroco Vintage worsted in 5134 Sour Cherry (3½ oz/218 yds) (Color B)
- G hook
- 14 bottle caps (can be ordered from Bernoulli Brew Werks)
- Sewing needle
- Sewing thread, gray
- Awl or ice pick
- Stitch marker

Basket Bottom

Rnd 1: Make a slip knot using color A. Ch 4, join into ring with a sl st. Sc 6 sts into the ring. Place a sm in the last st. Remove and place the sm in the last st of every rnd.

Rnd 2: Sc 2 into each sc. (12 sc)

Rnd 3: *Sc 2 in next sc, 1 sc in next sc. Repeat from * across the rnd. (18 sc)

Rnd 4: *Sc 2 in next sc, sc in each of next 2 sc. Repeat from * across the rnd. (24 sc)

Rnd 5: *Sc 2 in next sc, sc in each of next 3 sc. Repeat from * across the rnd. (30 sc)

Rnd 6: *Sc 2 in next sc, sc in each of next 4 sc. Repeat from * across the rnd. (36 sc)

Rnd 7: *Sc 2 in next sc, sc in each of next 5 sc. Repeat from * across the rnd. (42 sc)

Rnd 8: *Sc 2 in next sc, sc in each of next 6 sc. Repeat from * across the rnd. (48 sc)

Rnd 9: *Sc 2 in next sc, sc in each of next 7 sc. Repeat from * across the rnd. (54 sc)

Rnd 10: *Sc 2 in next sc, sc in each of next 8 sc. Repeat from * across the rnd. (60 sc)

Rnd 11: *Sc 2 in next sc, sc in each of next 9 sc. Repeat from * across the rnd. (66 sc)

Rnd 12: *Sc 2 in next sc, sc in each of next 10 sc. Repeat from * across the rnd. (72 sc)

Rnd 13: *Sc 2 in next sc, sc in each of next 11 sc. Repeat from * across the rnd. (78 sc)

Rnd 14: *Sc 2 in next sc, sc in each of next 12 sc. Repeat from * across the rnd. (84 sc)

Basket Side

Continue with color A for 3 rnds without increasing. Break yarn and join color B. Sc 10 rnds with color B. Break yarn and join color A. Sc 3 rnds with color A. Break yarn and work in ends.

Embellishment

Using an awl or ice pick, pierce three evenly spaced holes along the edge of each bottle cap. Making sure bottle caps are evenly spaced, sew them onto the color B band.

tulip time

FINISHED MEASUREMENTS: 5½-in. wide by 4½-in. high; filet 3-in. high
GAUGE: 4 sc = 1 inch (before felting)

Germany and Holland hold a special place in my heart. I lived in Germany for 3 years and later traveled to Holland and Germany on business. I love the "old world" feel over there—you feel as if you are stepping back in time. I created this pattern to give you that feel, but with a modern twist of felting the under basket. Layering the filet crochet with the smaller crocheted tulips gives it that "old world" feel.

YARN

MEDIUM   LACE

MATERIALS & TOOLS

- 1 skein Cascade 220 yarn in 9640 Green Agate (3½ oz/220 yds) (color A)
- 1 skein Cascade 220 yarn in 2442 Fog Hatt (3½ oz/220 yds) (color B)
- 1 ball Aunt Lydia's Classic Crochet Thread in 154-492 Burgundy (size $^{10}/_{350}$ yds)
- I hook
- C hook
- 0 hook
- Jumbo tapestry needle (such as Clover)
- Sewing thread to match tulip color
- Sewing needle
- Stitch markers
- Laundry bag
- Plastic grocery bag
- Pins

Bottom

Work first st of each rnd in same st as joining sl st. Do not turn.

Rnd 1: With color A and I hook ch 4; join with sl st in first ch to form ring. Work 8 sc in ring; join with sl st in first sc. (8 sc)

Rnd 2: Ch 1, 2 sc in each sc around. Join with sl st in first sc. (16 sc)

Rnd 3: Ch 1, *sc in next sc, 2 sc in next sc.* Repeat between the * 8 times. Join with sl st in first sc. (24 sc)

Rnd 4: Ch 1, *sc in next 2 sc, 2 sc in next sc.* Repeat between the * 8 times. Join with sl st in first sc. (32 sc)

Rnd 5: Ch 1, *sc in next 3 sc, 2 sc in next sc.* Repeat between the * 8 times. Join with sl st in first sc. (40 sc)

Rnd 6: Ch 1, *sc in next 4 sc, 2 sc in next sc.* Repeat between the * 8 times. Join with sl st in first sc. (48 sc)

Rnd 7: Ch 1, *sc in next 5 sc, 2 sc in next sc.* Repeat between the * 8 times. Join with sl st in first sc. (56 sc)

Rnd 8: Ch 1, *sc in next 6 sc, 2 sc in next sc.* Repeat between the * 8 times. Join with sl st in first sc. (64 sc)

Rnd 9: Ch 1, *sc in next 7 sc, 2 sc in next sc.* Repeat between the * 8 times. Join with sl st in first sc. (72 sc)

Rnd 10: Ch 1, *sc in next 17 sc, 2 sc in next sc.* Repeat between the * 4 times. Join with sl st in first sc. (76 sc)

Side

Rnd 11: Ch 1 and turn. FPsc around each sc. Join with sl st in first sc.

Rnd 12: Ch 1 and turn. Work into tops of sts of rnd 11. Sc in each sc around. Join with sl st in first sc.

Rnd 13: Ch 1. Sc in each sc around, working 1 sc2tog to decrease 1 st anywhere in the rnd. Join with sl st in first sc. (75 sc) When you do this dec rnd, make sure to dec in a different place on the rnd each time to even out the decreases.

Rnd 14: Ch 1, sc in each sc around. Join with sl st in first sc. (75 sc)

Rnds 15–20: Rep last 2 rnds 3 times. (72 sc)

Rnds 21–37: Ch 1. Sc in each sc around. Join with sl st in first sc. Fasten off. Weave ends in very well.

Felting

1: Place the basket in a laundry bag with a zipper. Wash with hot water and cold water rinse to felt. You may need to wash this about 3 times to felt it enough. Check after each wash cycle.

2: When the amount of felting that you like has been reached and the size of the basket is approximately the finished size of my basket, you are finished felting it.

3: Stuff a plastic grocery bag inside to shape while drying. Allow to dry.

Filet Sleeve

Row 1: With color B and C hook ch 105. Join to first ch with sl st to form a ring. Be careful to not twist it!

Row 2: Ch 4 (counts as first dc and ch 1). *Skip next ch and dc in next ch, ch 1.* Repeat between the * around. End row with sl st in third ch of starting ch 4. (52 open blocks)

Rows 3–11: Ch 4 (counts as first dc and ch 1). Dc in next dc, ch 1. *Dc in next dc, ch 1.* Repeat between * around. Join with sl st to third ch of starting ch 4. (52 open blocks) Fasten off. Weave in tails.

Tulips

Use Color C and 0 size hook; make 6.

Row 1: Ch 5. Skip first ch and sc in remaining chs. (4 sc)

Row 2: Ch 1 and turn. 2 sc in first sc. Sc in next 2, 2 sc in last sc. (6 sc)

Row 3: Ch 1 and turn. 2 sc in first sc. Sc in each of next 4 sc. 2 sc in last sc. (8 sc)

Rows 4–5: Ch 1 and turn. Sc in each across. (8 sc)

Row 6: Ch 1 and turn. 2 sc in first sc, sc in each of next 6 sc, 2 sc in last sc. (10 sc)

Rows 7–8: Ch 1 and turn. Sc in each across. (10 sc)

Row 9: Ch 1 and turn. 2 sc in first sc, sc in each of next 8 sc, sc in last sc. (12 sc)

Rows 10–11: Ch 1 and turn. Sc in each across. (12 sc)

Row 12: Ch 1 and turn. 2 sc in first sc. Sc in each of next 10 sc, 2 sc in last sc. (14 sc)

Rows 13–15: Ch 1 and turn. Sc in each sc across. (14 sc)

Row 16: Ch 1 and turn. Sc in next 4 sc. Leave remaining sts unworked. (4 sc for point of tulip)

Row 17: Ch 1 and turn. Sc in 4 sc. (4 sc for point of tulip)

Row 18: Ch 1 and turn. Sc in first 2 sc. Dec in next 2 sc. (3 sc)

Row 19: Ch 1 and turn. Dec in all 8 sc by pulling up a loop in all 3, YO, and through all loops. End.

Middle Petal/Point

Row 16: With first "petal/point" on the right side, insert hook in next sc from row 15. Join. Ch 1. Sc in same space as joining. Sc in next 4 sc. Leave remaining sts unworked. (5 sc)

Row 17: Ch 1 and turn. Dec in first 2 sc. Sc in next. Dec in last 2 sc. (3 sc)

Row 18: Ch 1 and turn. Sc in each sc. (3 sc)

Row 19: Ch 1 and turn. Dec in all 3. End.

With two "petals/points" on the right side, repeat instructions for last petal starting with Row 16. End.

Weave in tails. Evenly space the tulips on the filet crochet band. Pin in place. Hand-sew the tulips to the filet crocheted band. Slip band over the felted basket.

topsy-turvy tool tote basket

FINISHED MEASUREMENTS: 8½-in. wide by 5-in. high   **GAUGE:** 2 sc = 1¾ inch

Do you ever have to search your house for your knitting needles or just the right crochet hook because you forgot where you left them? Does your ball of yarn roll across the floor when you knit or crochet—or worse, go under the couch to meet all the dust bunnies that live there? If you answered yes to any of these questions, then this basket is for you! Turn the basket upside down over your yarn and pull the tail through the hole to prevent an escape while you work. Sewing button plackets and cuffs from shirts onto the basket creates plenty of spaces to store your tools, whether the basket is upright or upside down. Thus, the Topsy-Turvy Tool Tote!

MATERIALS & TOOLS

- 14 notches of wool strips (each notch is 3 x 60 in.)
- Q hook
- Sewing thread to match fabric (I used medium gray)
- Sewing needle
- Jumbo tapestry needle (such as Clover)
- 7 cuffs from wool shirts
- 1 button placket from a wool shirt
- 7 buttons
- Stitch markers (such as Clover Wonder Clip)

Crocheted by Debbie Decker

Wool

Snip and rip or use a cutter to cut the strips of wool into ½-inch by 60-inch pieces. Fold over the end of the strip about 1 inch and cut a slit in the center of the strip about ½-inch long. Repeat this with the new strip to be joined. Lay the new strip on top of the old strip with the tails facing in opposite directions. Grab the tail of the new strip and insert it through the old strip from underneath to the top, going through both slits. Pull the old and new strips in opposite directions until a knot forms. Continue to join strips as needed. To reduce the bulk of the fabric, you can cut the corners off the tops of the strips right above the slits.

Basket

Rnd 1: (RS) Ch 2, 9 sc in second ch from hook; do not join, place sm.

Rnd 2: 2 sc in each sc around. (18 sc)

Rnd 3: Sc in each sc around. (18 sc)

Rnd 4: 2 sc in each sc around. (36 sc)

Rnds 5–11: Sc in each sc around. (36 sc)

Rnd 12: Sl st in next sc to end. Taper tails from end of tail toward the basket. This will make it easier to weave in the tails. Weave in tails.

Embellishments

1: Fold cuffs over the top edge with the pointed side out and pointing down. Place evenly around the top edge. On the inside edge, the bottom of the cuff should be approximately even with the second from the top row sc. Pin in place. Hand stitch the bottom edge of the cuff on the inside of the basket.

2: Pin the button side of the button placket to the inside edge, matching the top edge of the basket with the top edge of the button placket. Hand stitch the button placket to the sides of the cuffs only. Use a backstitch to stitch in place. You will be leaving the bottom and top edge open to insert tools.

3: Place the buttonhole side of the button placket on the outside top edge of the basket. Ends will be hidden under one of the cuffs. Pin in place just under the top edge. Sew the two raw edges of the button placket with thread. Fold the cuff down over the button placket. Sew through the button placket and the cuff with thread to attach a button. Secure and knot through the basket to hold the cuff in place. Repeat around for remaining cuffs.

Place your tools in the open parts of the button placket on the inside and the outside of the basket.

Tiny wire basket

FINISHED MEASUREMENTS: 1-in. wide by 1½-in. high   **GAUGE:** 2 st = ¼ inch

Don't let the size of this basket fool you. Despite its size, it has "big" potential. Linda has a beautiful woven silver basket that she wears as a pendant. I have admired this so much over the years. Now, I can have a basket pendant too! I don't like to make woven baskets, so crocheting this little basket was the perfect answer for me. These are also the perfect size to use in doll houses.

YARN

LACE

MATERIALS & TOOLS

- 15 yds 26-gauge turquoise ParaWire
- C hook
- Wire cutters
- Large-eye sharp needle

Basket

Rnd 1: Ch 2 (first ch counts as first sc). 5 sc in second ch from the hook. Join with sl st to the first ch.

Rnd 2: Ch 2 (counts as first dc). Dc in starting st. 2 dc in each sc around. (12 dc). Join to the top of the ch 2 with a sl st.

Rnd 3: Ch 3 (counts as first tr st). Crocheting in the back loop only, tr st in each dc around. Join with sl st to ch 3. (12 tr st). Do not end.

Handle

Ch 10 for handle. Join with sl st directly across the top of the basket from the start of the handle. End. Use a sharp large-eye needle to weave in the ends. Cut ends with wire cutters.

1970s shag

What a decade the '70s were! Shag carpet was all the rage and all houseware items came in antique gold, avocado green, rust, and chocolate brown. This basket is a tribute to the swinging 1970s and shag carpet, all in decade-correct colorways. Does anyone still use shag carpet in their home?

YARN

MEDIUM

MATERIALS & TOOLS

- 1 skein Red Heart Super Saver Yarn in 4365 Coffee Fleck (5 oz/260 yds)

- I hook

- Stitch marker

- 6-in. pieces of yarn in earth tones

Crocheted and embellished by Priscilla Pietz

Note: Hold two strands together throughout while crocheting.

Bottom

Rnd 1: Make a slipknot. Ch 4, join into ring with a sl st. Sc 6 into the ring. Place a sm in the last st. Remove and place sm in last st of every rnd.

Rnd 2: Increase by crocheting 2 sc into every sc. (12 sc)

Rnd 3: *Sc 2 in next sc, 1 sc in next sc. Repeat from * across the rnd. (18 sc)

Rnd 4: *Sc 2 in next sc, 2 sc in next sc. Repeat from * across the rnd. (24 sc)

Rnd 5: *Sc 2 in next sc, 3 sc in next sc. Repeat from * across the rnd. (30 sc)

Rnd 6: *Sc 2 in next sc, 4 sc in next sc. Repeat from * across the rnd. (36 sc)

Rnd 7: *Sc 2 in next sc, 5 sc in next sc. Repeat from * across the rnd. (42 sc)

Rnd 8: *Sc 2 in next sc, 6 sc in next sc. Repeat from * across the rnd. (48 sc)

Rnd 9: *Sc 2 in next sc, 7 sc in next sc. Repeat from * across the rnd. (54 sc)

Rnd 10: *Sc 2 in next sc, 8 sc in next sc. Repeat from * across the rnd. (60 sc)

Side

*Sc in the back loop of each sc across the rnd. Repeat from * until basket side measures 3½ inches. End with sl st, break yarn, and work in ends.

Embellishment

Starting at the bottom of the basket side, insert crochet hook into one of the front loops going from the bottom to the top. Fold a piece of 6-inch earth-tone yarn in half. Pull this partway through the loop on the basket. Using the crochet hook, pull ends of the yarn pieces back through the loop you created. Tighten by hand. Repeat this in all but the top row of loops, working one rnd at a time from the bottom of the basket toward the top. If you take a break from embellishing the basket, leave the crochet hook in the next loop to be done to easily find where you left off.

picture this

I love to look at pictures of my loved ones, but I like to have the flexibility to change the pictures often and easily. With this basket, you can do that. The elastic makes it so easy to change the pictures whenever you like.

MATERIALS & TOOLS

- 3-ft x 30-in. red wool fabric
- N hook
- 2 pieces black elastic, ½-in. wide, or black elastic headbands (such as Scünci No-Slip Grip headbands, cut in 4 pieces, 2 pieces used)
- Heavy black thread
- Sewing needle
- Jumbo tapestry needle (such as Clover)
- Rotary cutter or fabric cutter

Wool

Snip and rip or use a cutter to cut the strips of wool into ½-inch by 60-inch pieces. Fold over the end of the strip about 1 inch and cut a slit in the center of the strip about ½-inch long. Repeat this with the new strip to be joined. Lay the new strip on top of the old strip with the tails facing in opposite directions. Grab the tail of the new strip and insert it through the old strip from underneath to the top, going through both slits. Pull the old and new strips in opposite directions until a knot forms. Continue to join strips as needed. To reduce the bulk of the fabric, you can cut the corners off the tops of the strips right above the slits.

Bottom

Row 1: Ch 20. Sc in second ch from hook and each remaining across. (19 sc)

Rows 2–12: Ch 1 turn. Sc in each sc across. (19 sc)

Sides

Row 1: Make slip knot on hook. Insert into base through the first opening of second row on the right side of the base. Go under the sc and come up in the next opening on the left side of the sc. YO and pull up a loop and pull through to the first opening. YO and pull through both loops on hook. Insert the hook into second hole, go under the sc to third hole. YO and pull loop through to second hole. YO and pull through both loops on hook. Repeat all the way around, going in each hole. Join with sl st to first sc.

Row 2: *Ch 1 and turn. Sc in each around.* Repeat between * around. Join with sl st to first sc. (52 sc)

Rows 3–7: Do not turn. Sc in next sc and in each sc around. Sl st in first sc.

Row 8: Do not turn. Sc in next sc and in each sc around. Sl st in first sc and next. End. Weave in tails.

Attach Elastic

Measure about 2 inches in from the side on the front or back of the basket. Using one piece of black elastic or the cut headband, tuck under the raw edge and sew right under the top edge to the red wool with heavy-duty black thread. Then tuck under the bottom raw edge and sew in place right on top of the bottom edge of the basket. Repeat on the other side. You could sew on two more to hold a 4 x 6-inch photo more securely. If you do that, measure 2 inches in from the other side and repeat instructions above. I only did the one to make it easier to slip a photo in and out and see more of the photo.

hundertwasser's spiral

FINISHED MEASUREMENTS: 8½-in. wide by 3½-in. high   **GAUGE:** 4 sc = 1 inch

Have you ever thought about changing your name or wondered what your parents were thinking when they named you? Whether Friedrich Stowasser pondered that is unclear, but he did choose to change his name. Abandoning his given name, he became Friedensreich Hundertwasser to the world of art. This very unconventional artist not only painted, but designed delightful Dr. Seuss-like buildings. Not liking straight lines, he was fascinated by spirals, which he viewed as a symbol of life and nature. The spiral in this unusual basket is a tribute to Hundertwasser's creative spirit.

YARN

MATERIALS & TOOLS

- 1 skein each Cascade 220 yarn (3½ oz/220 yds) in the following colors:
  - 9484 Stratosphere (color A)
  - 8895 Christmas Red (color B)
  - 8894 Christmas Green (color C)
  - 7828 Neon Yellow (color D)
  - 9570 Concord Grape (color E)
  - 9542 Blaze (color F)
- G hook
- Stitch marker

Note: Hold two strands together throughout. When changing from one color to the next color, with 2 loops of the old color on the hook, YO with the new color and pull through the loops.

Bottom

With color A, make a slip knot. Ch 4 and join into a ring with a sl st.

Rnd 1: 6 sc into ring. Place sm on the last sc—remove each rnd and place on the new last st.

Rnd 2: 2 sc in each sc. (12 sc)

Rnd 3: *2 sc in next sc, 1 sc in next sc. Repeat from * across the rnd. (18 sc)

Rnd 4: *2 sc in next sc, 1 sc in each of next 2 sc. Repeat from * across the rnd. (24 sc)

Rnd 5: *2 sc in next sc, 1 sc in each of next 3 sc. Repeat from * across the rnd. (30 sc)

Rnd 6: *2 sc in next sc, 1 sc in each of next 4 sc. Repeat from * across the rnd. (36 sc)

Rnd 7: *2 sc in next sc, 1 sc in each of next 5 sc. Repeat from * across the rnd. (42 sc)

Rnd 8: *2 sc in next sc, 1 sc in each of next 6 sc. Repeat from * across the rnd. (48 sc)

Rnd 9: *2 sc in next sc, 1 sc in each of next 7 sc. Repeat from * across the rnd. (54 sc)

Rnd 10: *2 sc in next sc, 1 sc in each of next 8 sc. Repeat from * across the rnd. (60 sc)

Rnd 11: *2 sc in next sc, 1 sc in each of next 9 sc. Repeat from * across the rnd. (66 sc)

Rnd 12: *2 sc in next sc, 1 sc in each of next 10 sc. Repeat from * across the rnd. (72 sc)

Sides

Rnd 1: Sc 12 working through back loops for the entire rnd. Sc 12 of color B, sc 12 of color C, sc 12 of color D, sc 12 of color E, and sc 12 of color F.

Rnd 2: Continue following the color order through both loops. The next color will be there to pick up and crochet when the color being worked with is completed. It will appear as if there is a longer section as one rnd is finished, because that same color will be used for the beginning of the next rnd.

Rnd 3: Continue following the color order, increase 1 sc in the first sc of each color section. (78 sc)

Rnds 4–5: Continue following the color order.

Rnd 6: Same as rnd 3. (84 sc)

Rnds 7–8: Continue following the color order.

Rnd 9: Same as rnd 3. (90 sc)

Rnds 10–11: Continue following the color order.

Rnd 12: Same as rnd 3. (96 sc)

Rnds 13–14: Continue following the color order.

Rnd 15: Same as rnd 3. (102 sc) Break yarns and work in ends.

hook, yarn, crochet

FINISHED MEASUREMENTS: 10-in. wide by 5-in. high   **GAUGE:** 3½ sc = 1 inch

"And all I ask is a tall ship and a star to steer her by."

It's funny where inspiration comes from. Believe it or not, this line from the poem "Sea Fever" by John Masefield was the inspiration for this basket. Let's face it, as crocheters, isn't all we ask for nothing more than a hook, some yarn, and perhaps a pattern to take us on an adventure of creativity?

YARN

MATERIALS & TOOLS

- 1 skein Red Heart Super Saver yarn 380 Windsor Blue (7 oz/364 yds) (color A)
- 1 skein Red Heart Super Saver yarn 624 Tea Leaf (7 oz/364 yds) (color B)
- I hook
- Stitch marker

Note: When not being used, the other color in the basket will be carried by crocheting over this color. Because there is no tension on this color, periodically gently pull on it, so that it does not show through the work. When coming to a color change, YO with the new color when there are 2 loops left on your hook of the previous color. The two yarns get tangles quickly. Make sure to untangle them periodically. If you run out of the yarn you are carrying, just start crocheting over the new piece of yarn. Use two strands of yarn throughout the basket.

Rnd 1: Make a slip knot with color A, leaving a 9-yard tail. Ch 4, join into ring with a sl st. Sc 6 sts into the ring while carrying the tail yarn. Place a sm in the last st. Remove and replace this sm in the last st of every rnd. Continue to crochet over the tail to maintain the correct gauge throughout.

Rnd 2: Sc 2 in each of 6 sc around. (12 sc)

Rnd 3: *Sc 2 in next sc, 1 sc in next sc. Repeat from * across the rnd. (18 sc)

Rnd 4: *Sc 2 in next sc, 1 sc in each of next 2 sc. Repeat from * across the rnd. (24 sc)

Rnd 5: *Sc 2 in next sc, 1 sc in each of next 3 sc. Repeat from * across the rnd. (30 sc)

Rnd 6: *Sc 2 in next sc, 1 sc in each of next 4 sc. Repeat from * across the rnd. (36 sc)

Rnd 7: *Sc 2 in next sc, 1 sc in each of next 5 sc. Repeat from * across the rnd. (42 sc)

Rnd 8: *Sc 2 in next sc, 1 sc in each of next 6 sc. Repeat from * across the rnd. (48 sc)

Rnd 9: *Sc 2 in next sc, 1 sc in each of next 7 sc. Repeat from * across the rnd. (54 sc)

Rnd 10: *Sc 2 in next sc, 1 sc in each of next 8 sc. Repeat from * across the rnd. (60 sc)

Rnd 11: *Sc 2 in next sc, 1 sc in each of next 9 sc. Repeat from * across the rnd. (66 sc)

Rnd 12: *Sc 2 in next sc, 1 sc in each of next 10 sc. Repeat from * across the rnd. (72 sc)

Rnd 13: *Sc 2 in next sc, 1 sc in each of next 11 sc. Repeat from * across the rnd. (78 sc)

Rnd 14: *Sc 2 in next sc, 1 sc in each of next 12 sc. Repeat from * across the rnd. (84 sc)

Rnd 15: *Sc 2 in next sc, 1 sc in each of next 13 sc. Repeat from * across the rnd. (90 sc)

Rnd 16: *Sc 2 in next sc, 1 sc in each of next 14 sc.* Repeat between the * across the rnd. (96 sc) Stop carrying color A and start carrying color B if making the small basket.

Rnd 17: *Sc in each of next 15 sts, 2 sc in next st.* Repeat between the * 3 times more. Crochet to the end of the rnd. (100 sc) Start working from chart A, reading from right to left. The background will be color B, with lettering in color A. On the second to last band, the colors will be reversed using chart B. Sl st the last st. Break yarns and work in ends.

Chart B

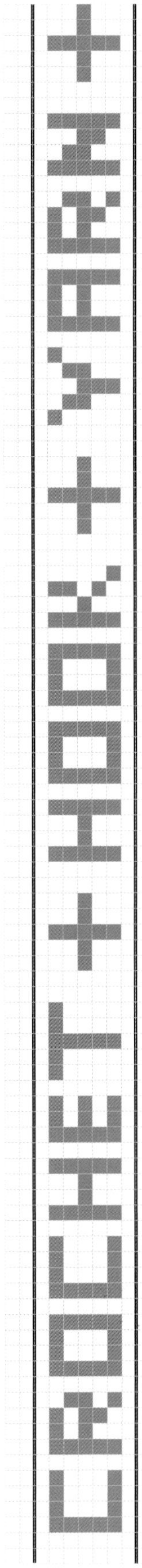

CROCHET + HOOK + YARN +

Chart A

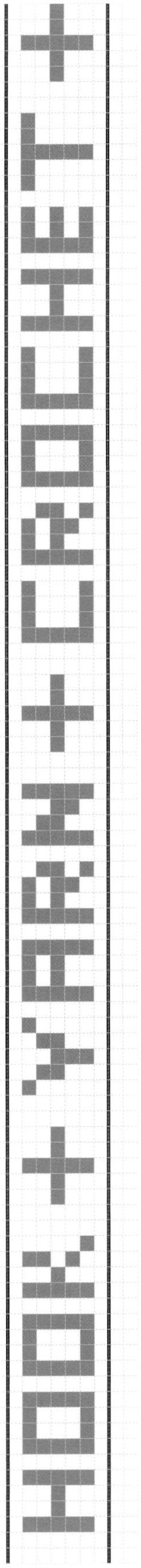

HOOK + YARN + CROCHET +

One box equals one stitch.

loopy pet bed

Our pet bed basket may not be suitable for pets such as my daughter's pet tortoise Hannibal or your beloved parakeet, but it will be perfect for your furry little darling canine or feline. If you are the proud owner of a Great Dane or an exotic member of the cat family, just add more rows to the base to create a larger bed. Can't you just imagine them snuggling into their very own bed, crocheted with love?

YARN

MATERIALS & TOOLS

- 1 16-oz bag each Wool Novelty Company cotton weaving loops in the following colors:
  - Green (yellow green)
  - Lavender
  - Red
  - Medium blue
  - Yellow
  - Dark blue
  - Orange
  - Pink (Reverse the last two if you think that looks better.)
- Size 19 hook
- Stitch marker
- 2 yards 60-in.-wide wool fabric, washed and dried
- Matching thread
- Stuffing

Make Loopy Yarn

Join loops as needed following the order of color listed in the materials list, starting with green. Crochet through one color before switching to the next color. Make about 5 yards to start with. To make the loopy yarn, take one loop and insert it into another. Insert the end of that loop into itself and pull tight. Two loops are now joined. Insert another loop into one of the joined loops and again insert the end of this loop into itself and pull tight. Repeat as needed.

Bottom

Make a slip knot, ch 4, and join into ring with a sl st.

Rnd 1: 6 sc into ring. Place sm on the last sc—remove each rnd and place on the new last st.

Rnd 2: 2 sc in each sc. (12 sc)

Rnd 3: *2 sc in next sc, 1 sc in next sc. Repeat from * across the rnd. (18 sc)

Rnd 4: *2 sc in next sc, sc in each of next 2 sc. Repeat from * across the rnd. (24 sc)

Rnd 5: *2 sc in next sc, sc in each of next 3 sc. Repeat from * across the rnd. (30 sc)

Rnd 6: *2 sc in next sc, sc in each of next 4 sc. Repeat from * across the rnd. (36 sc)

Rnd 7: *2 sc in next sc, sc in each of next 5 sc. Repeat from * across the rnd. (42 sc)

Rnd 8: *2 sc in next sc, sc in each of next 6 sc. Repeat from * across the rnd. (48 sc)

Rnd 9: *2 sc in next sc, sc in each of next 7 sc. Repeat from * across the rnd. (54 sc)

Rnd 10: *2 sc in next sc, sc in each of next 8 sc. Repeat from * across the rnd. (60 sc)

Rnd 11: *2 sc in next sc, sc in each of next 9 sc. Repeat from * across the rnd. (66 sc)

Rnd 12: *2 sc in next sc, sc in each of next 10 sc. Repeat from * across the rnd. (72 sc)

Rnd 13: *2 sc in next sc, sc in each of next 11 sc. Repeat from * across the rnd. (78 sc)

Rnd 14: *2 sc in next sc, sc in each of next 12 sc. Repeat from * across the rnd. (84 sc)

Sides

Work even for 26 rows. Fold over to the outside and sew down.

Cushion

1: From the wool fabric, cut two 22-inch circles. Cut two 10 x 36½-inch pieces.

2: Sew the short sides together using a ½-inch seam allowance. This is the side piece.

3: Pin the side piece to one of the circles with RS together. Clip curves. Iron the seam. Sew the other side seam.

4: Pin the other circle to the side piece with RS together and sew, leaving a 6-inch opening.

5: Turn RS out and stuff as desired. Hand-sew opening with matching thread. Insert into basket.

bird's nest

FINISHED MEASUREMENTS: 8-in. wide by 5½-in. high   **GAUGE:** 4 sc = 1 inch

My father could always be counted on to give us the most random book as a Christmas gift. One year, I tore into a very heavy package to discover an encyclopedic book on birds of the world. I had never expressed any great interest in birds, but through enjoying that book's beautiful color illustrations, I developed a fondness for those (mostly) diminutive engineering marvels.

YARN

MATERIALS & TOOLS

- 1 skein each Cascade 220 yarn (3½ oz/220 yds) in the following colors:
  - 9557 Dark Chocolate (color A)
  - 2440 Vinci (color B)
  - 9634 Aqua Haze (color C)
  - 8891 Cyan Blue (color D)
  - 8505 White (color E)
  - 9463B Gold (color F)
  - 2429 Ireland (color G)
  - 2445 Shire (color H)
- G hook
- Stitch marker
- #18 tapestry needle
- Dark blue floss

Note: Hold two strands together for crocheted portion of the basket. Use one strand for the cross stitch.

Bottom

Holding one strand each of color A and B together, make a slip knot. Ch 4 and join into a ring with a sl st.

Rnd 1: 6 sc into ring. Place sm on the last sc. Remove each rnd and place on the new last st.

Rnd 2: 2 sc in each sc. (12 sc)

Rnd 3: *2 sc in next sc, 1 sc in next sc. Repeat from * across the rnd. (18 sc)

Rnd 4: *2 sc in next sc, sc in each of next 2 sc. Repeat from * across the rnd. (24 sc)

Rnd 5: *2 sc in next sc, sc in each of next 3 sc. Repeat from * across the rnd. (30 sc)

Rnd 6: *2 sc in next sc, sc in each of next 4 sc. Repeat from * across the rnd. (36 sc)

Rnd 7: *2 sc in next sc, sc in each of next 5 sc. Repeat from * across the rnd. (42 sc)

Rnd 8: *2 sc in next sc, sc in each of next 6 sc. Repeat from * across the rnd. (48 sc)

Rnd 9: *2 sc in next sc, sc in each of next 7 sc. Repeat from * across the rnd. (54 sc)

Rnd 10: *2 sc in next sc, sc in each of next 8 sc. Repeat from * across the rnd. (60 sc)

Rnd 11: *2 sc in next sc, sc in each of next 9 sc. Repeat from * across the rnd. (66 sc)

Rnd 12: *2 sc in next sc, sc in each of next 10 sc. Repeat from * across the rnd. (72 sc)

Rnd 13: *2 sc in next sc, sc in each of next 11 sc. Repeat from * across the rnd. (78 sc)

Rnd 14: *2 sc in next sc, sc in each of next 12 sc. Repeat from * across the rnd. (84 sc)

Rnd 15: *2 sc in next sc, sc in each of next 13 sc. Repeat from * across the rnd. (90 sc)

Sides

Rnd 1: Sc 1 rnd with no increases.

Rnd 2: Sc 1 rnd with no increases, crocheting into the back loop. Continue crocheting in the back loops for the rest of the nest portion of the basket.

Rnd 3: *2 sc next sc, sc in each of next 14 sc. Repeat from * across the rnd. (96 sc)

Rnds 4–5: Sc even.

Rnd 6: *2 sc next sc, sc in each of next 15 sc. Repeat from * across the rnd. (102 sc)

Rnd 7: Sc even.

Rnd 8: *Sc2tog, sc in each of next 15 sc. Repeat from * across the rnd. (96 sc) Break yarn and join color C.

Rnd 9: Sc even in the back loops.

Rnds 10–20: Sc even through both loops. Break yarn and join color H.

Rnd 21: Sc 1 rnd even. Break yarn and work in ends.

Nest

Cut pieces of color A and B approximately 3 to 4 inches in length. Tie one strand of each color to every other front loop of the nest. Unravel some of the strands to give it a more natural nest look.

Embellishment

Using colors D through H, follow the chart below to cross stitch in the birds, leaves, and eggs. Using color A, make a French knot for the eye of the bird. Using all six strands of dark blue floss, back stitch in the wing detail following the chart.

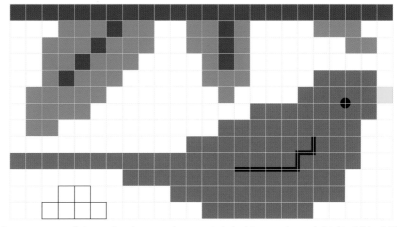

Repeat pattern 4 times. One box equals one stitch. In this sample, each bird is 6½" x 2¼".

flower garden

FINISHED MEASUREMENTS: 5-in. wide by 2⅞-in. high   **GAUGE:** 4 sc = 1 inch
FINISHED FLOWER = 1¼ inch

As I am writing this, it is summertime in St. Louis. In front of our house is a blanket of bright flowers. The contrast against our white frame house is beautiful! We have to have the yellow and orange variety of marigolds. Let's not forget the pinks, reds, and purples of the zinnias. Last but not least, my favorite—the sunflowers. Think of the bright colors of summer as you crochet this basket.

YARN

MATERIALS & TOOLS

- 1 skein Cascade 220 yarn in 9640 Green Agate (3½ oz/220 yds) (color A)
- 1 skein each DMC Tapestry yarn (8.7 yds) in the following colors:
  - 7341, grass green (color B)
  - 7725, golden (color C)
  - 7138, dark red (color D)
  - 7603, rose pink (color E)
  - 7947, orange (color F)
- I hook
- B hook
- Jumbo tapestry needle (such as Clover)
- Sewing thread to match basket color
- Sewing needle
- Laundry bag
- Stitch marker

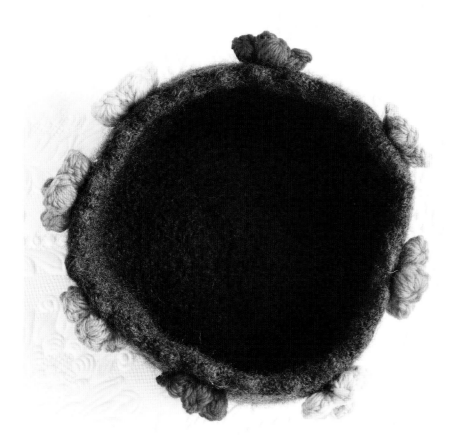

Side

Rnds 13–24: Ch 1. Sc in each sc around. (72 sc)

Rnd 25: *Sl st in next sc, sl st in next sc, ch 3, sl st in next sc. Repeat from * across the rnd. End. Weave in tails.

Felting

Place this basket in a laundry bag with a zipper. Wash with hot water and rinse with cold water to felt. You may need to wash this about 3 times to felt it enough. Check after each wash cycle. When the amount of felting that you like has been reached and the size of the basket is approximately the finished size of my basket you are finished felting it. Stuff a plastic grocery bag inside to shape while drying. Allow to dry.

Flowers

Use a B hook. Make two of each color flower (colors C through F)—eight total.

1: With green yarn (color B), ch 2. 5 sc in second ch from hook. Join with sl st to first sc. Fasten off. Weave in tails before proceeding with petals.

2: Join flower color to green in any sc.

3: Ch 2, YO, insert hook in same sc, and pull up a loop, (YO, insert hook in same st, and pull up a loop) 4 times, YO, and draw through 11 loops on the hook. First bobble stitch is now completed.

4: (Ch 3, and sl st in next sc. Ch 2. YO and insert hook in same sc. Pull up a loop, [YO, insert hook in same st, and pull up a loop] 4 times. YO and draw through 11 loops on the hook.) 3 times.

5: Ch 3 and join in first ch of first petal. Fasten off. Make five petals. Make a total of eight flowers using the colors you like. Weave in tails.

6: Pin flowers evenly around the top edge in a manner that is pleasing to you. Hand sew flowers to the outside of the top of the basket with sewing thread.

Basket

With color A, ch 4 and form a ring with a sl st.

Rnd 1: 6 sc into ring. Place sm on the last sc. Remove each rnd and place on the new last stitch. (6 sc)

Rnd 2: 2 sc in each sc around. (12 sc)

Rnd 3: *2 sc in next sc, 1 sc in next sc. Repeat from * across the rnd. (18 sc)

Rnd 4: *2 sc in next sc, sc in each of next 2 sc. Repeat from * across the rnd. (24 sc)

Rnd 5: *2 sc in next sc, sc in each of next 3 sc. Repeat from * across the rnd. (30 sc)

Rnd 6: *2 sc in next sc, sc in each of next 4 sc. Repeat from * across the rnd. (36 sc)

Rnd 7: Ch 1. *2 sc in first dc. Sc in each of next 5 dc. Repeat from * across the rnd. Join with sl st to ch 1. (42 sc)

Rnd 8: Ch 1. *2 sc in first sc. Sc in each of next 6 sc. Repeat from * across the rnd. Join with sl st to top of ch 1. (48 sc)

Rnd 9: Ch 1. *2 sc in first sc. Sc in each of next 7 sc. Repeat from * across the rnd. Join with sl st to top of ch 1. (54 sc)

Rnd 10: Ch 1. *2 sc in first sc. Sc in each of next 8 sc. Repeat from * across the rnd. Join with sl st to top of ch 1. (60 sc)

Rnd 11: Ch 1. * 2 sc in first sc. Sc in each of next 9 sc. Repeat from * across the rnd. Join with sl st to top of ch 1. (66 sc)

Rnd 12: Ch 1. *2 sc in first sc. Sc in each of next 10 sc. Repeat from * across the rnd. Join with sl st to top of ch 1. (72 sc)

basket weave basket

Like baskets, but you don't like basket weaving? That's me. This basket will give you the look of a woven basket without having to weave a traditional basket. This one is crocheted using a light-colored neutral yarn to accentuate the woven pattern. The stitches that are used to create this wonderful woven look are the back post double crochet and the front post double crochet. "Weave" a basket today!

YARN

MATERIALS & TOOLS

- 2 skeins Chunky Monkey Yarn light gray (4 oz/75 yds)
- J hook
- Jumbo tapestry needle

Crocheted by Melissa Polumbus

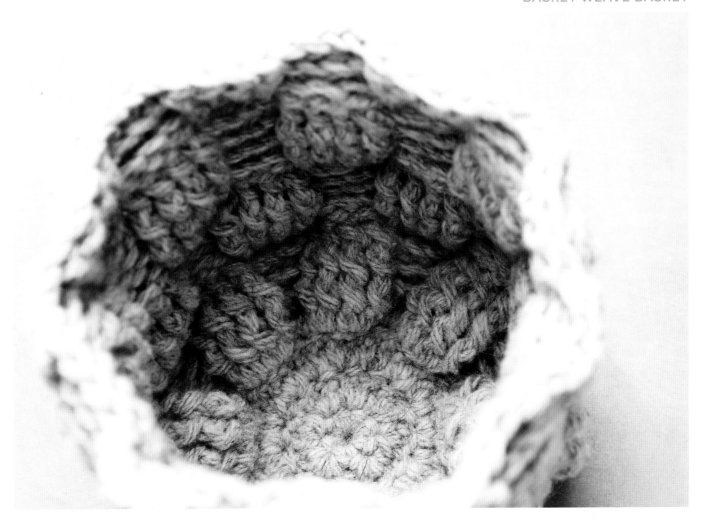

Basket

Rnd 1: Make a magic ring. Ch 1. 7 sc in ring. Pull ring tight. Join with sl st to first sc.

Rnd 2: Ch 1, 2 dc in first sc and in each sc around. Join with sl st to top of beginning sc. (14 dc)

Rnd 3: Ch 2. 2 dc in first sc and in each around. Join with sl st to top of beginning ch 2. (28 dc)

Rnd 4: Ch 2. 2 dc in first dc and in each around. Join with sl st to top of beginning ch 2. (56 dc)

Rnd 5: Ch 2. Work FPdc around each of first 4 dc, work BPdc around each of next 4 dc, work FPdc around each of next 4 dc, work BPdc around each of next 4 dc, work FPdc around each of next 4 dc, work BPdc around each of next 4 dc, work FPdc around each of next 4 dc. Join with sl st to top of beginning ch 2. (28 FPdc, 28 BPdc)

Rnds 6–7: Ch 2. Work FPdc around each FPdc and work BPdc around each all the way around. Join with sl st to top of beginning ch 2.

Rnd 8: Ch 2. Work BPdc around each FPdc and work FPdc around each BPdc all the way around. Join with sl st to top of beginning ch 2.

Rnds 9–11: Ch 2. Work BPdc around each BPdc and work FPdc around each FPdc all the way around. Join with sl st to top of beginning ch 2.

Rnd 12: Ch 2. Work FPdc around each BPdc and work BPdc around each FPdc all the way around. Join with sl st to top of beginning ch 2.

Rnds 13–15: Ch 2. Work FPdc around each FPdc and work BPdc around each BPdc all the way around. Join with sl st to top of beginning ch 2.

Rnds 16–19: Repeat instructions for rnds 8–11.

Sl st in first dc of next rnd to end. Cut yarn and weave in the tail.

put a lid on it!

You won't lose anything with this basket. The lid will keep everything contained and hidden from curious eyes. You won't even lose the lid, because the lid is attached!

YARN

MATERIALS & TOOLS

- 1 skein Bonnie Braid macrame cord in Tan (6mm/100 yds)
- N hook
- Scissors
- Jumbo tapestry needle (such as Clover)
- Matches
- 4 1-in. vintage black buttons
- Matching thread
- Sewing needle

Bottom

Rnd 1: Make a magic ring. 6 sc in ring. Join with sl st to first sc.

Rnd 2: 2 sc in each around. (12 sc) Do not join.

Rnd 3: 2 sc in each around. (24 sc) Do not join.

Rnd 4: Ch 2 (counts as first dc). Dc in back loop of each sc. Dc in back loop of sc where there is the ch 2. Join with sl st to top of the ch 2. (24 dc)

Rnd 5: Ch 2 (counts as first dc). Dc in back loop of each dc. Join with sl st to top of ch 2. (24 dc) Do not end. Leave loop. You will come back to this to join the lid later.

Lid

I used the other end of the Bonnie Braid so I would not have to cut the basket loop.

Rnds 1–3: Repeat instructions from the basket.

Rnd 4: Join the lid by turning the lid upside down so WS is facing you. Take hook out and reinsert the hook into loop of lid from right to left.

Match up yarn from basket and loop on hook. YO with yarn from basket. Pull through loop of hook for sl st. Pull yarn tight from lid and yarn from basket. End. Cut yarn from basket and from the lid. Weave in tails with the jumbo tapestry needle. Pull tails very tight. Cut close to crocheting. Light match and burn the end. Quickly push burnt end under crocheting to secure. Repeat with other tails.

Buttons

Stack the buttons and sew on the lid using strong thread. I went from the top to the inside of the lid, back to the top with my thread. I tied my thread on top for an extra decorative touch.

easter parade

After the cold and seeming deadness of winter, what could be more thrilling than those first green shoots of spring bringing color back to the world? It's wonderful to see the little animals, such as rabbits and birds, begin to stir with the first blooms. This tribute to glorious spring sports a new growth of grass, bunnies, and chickens, along with colorful blossoms.

YARN

MATERIALS & TOOLS

- 1 skein each Cascade 220 yarn (3½ oz/220 yds) in the following colors:
  - 9407 Celery (color A)
  - 9461 Lime Heather (color B)
  - 8687 Butter (color C)
  - 2449 Peony Pink (color D)
  - 9453 Amethyst Heather (color E)
- F hook
- 2 yds ⅜-in.-wide yellow ribbon
- Stitch marker
- 2 metal bunny cookie cutters
- 2 metal chicken cookie cutters

> **Note:** Hold two strands together throughout the basket and flowers.

Bottom

Holding one strand each of color A and color B together, make a slip knot. Ch 4 and join into a ring with a sl st.

Rnd 1: 6 sc into ring. Place sm on the last sc—remove each rnd and place on the new last st.

Rnd 2: 2 sc in each sc. (12 sc)

Rnd 3: *2 sc in next sc, 1 sc in next sc. Repeat from * across the rnd. (18 sc)

Rnd 4: *2 sc in next sc, sc in each of next 2 sc. Repeat from * across the rnd. (24 sc)

Rnd 5: *2 sc in next sc, sc in each of next 3 sc. Repeat from * across the rnd. (30 sc)

Rnd 6: *2 sc in next sc, sc in each of next 4 sc. Repeat from * across the rnd. (36 sc)

Rnd 7: *2 sc in next sc, sc in each of next 5 sc. Repeat from * across the rnd. (42 sc)

Rnd 8: *2 sc in next sc, sc in each of next 6 sc. Repeat from * across the rnd. (48 sc)

Rnd 9: *2 sc in next sc, sc in each of next 7 sc. Repeat from * across the rnd. (54 sc)

Rnd 10: *2 sc in next sc, sc in each of next 8 sc. Repeat from * across the rnd. (60 sc)

Rnd 11: *2 sc in next sc, sc in each of next 9 sc. Repeat from * across the rnd. (66 sc)

Rnd 12: *2 sc in next sc, sc in each of next 10 sc. Repeat from * across the rnd. (72 sc)

Rnd 13: *2 sc in next sc, sc in each of next 11 sc. Repeat from * across the rnd. (78 sc)

Rnd 14: *2 sc in next sc, sc in each of next 12 sc. Repeat from * across the rnd. (84 sc)

Rnd 15: *2 sc in next sc, sc in each of next 13 sc. Repeat from * across the rnd. (90 sc)

Rnd 16: *2 sc in next sc, sc in each of next 14 sc. Repeat from * across the rnd. (96 sc)

Sides

Continuing with color A and color B, sc for 3 rnds going into the back loops. Break yarn and join color C. For the first rnd only, sc into the back loops only. Continuing with color C, sc for 17 rnds more.

Top Edging

Crocheting into back loops, *sl 1, sc 1, hdc 1, dc 1, tr 1, dc 1, hdc 1, sc.* Repeat between the * across the rnd. Break yarn and work in ends.

Grass

Using colors A and B together and working with basket upside down, start in the last front loop of the basket. *1 sl st in each of next 4 front loops, chain 7, sl st in back loops of the ch sts, sl st into the same front loop to secure the blade of grass. Repeat from * in all front loops of the grass portion of the basket.

Stems

Insert hook at the top of the grass between two sc. Make a slip knot with color A and B together; pull up the loop from the inside of the basket. Going up to the next row, reinsert the hook and pull up another loop from the inside and through the loop on the hook. Continue

in this manner until there are 14 surface chains for the stem. Break yarn and bring tail to the back. Work in ends. Crochet three stems more, spacing them 24 sc apart.

Flowers

Using color D, make a slip knot, ch 4, join into ring using a sl st. 5 sc in ring. 2 sc in each of 5 sc. (10 sc) Break yarn.

Using color E, join into any sc of the previous rnd using a sl st. Ch 3, *2 tr in next sc, ch 3, sl st in next sc, ch 3.* Repeat between the * 3 times more. 2 tr in next sc, ch 3, join into beginning of rnd with a sl st. There should be five petals. Break yarn, leaving a long tail. Use tail to sew each flower to the top of a stem.

Cookie Cutters

Using the 16 inches of ribbon, tie the cookie cutters to the basket. Make sure that the bunnies and chickens are "sitting" on the grass.

spring Trio

A tisket, a tasket, how about a spring basket? Spring is a time of re-birth and growth, and full of color. We always know that spring is right around the corner when we see the crocus, daffodils, and tulips pop their heads up from the frosty ground. Always such a welcome sight after the harshness of winter! I used bright colors for these spring baskets to rejoice in the season. Using a combination of tulle and netting (netting has larger holes and is coarser; tulle has smaller holes and is finer and softer) gives these baskets a softer look and feel. Tying bright green "grass" to the inside of the baskets adds to the feeling of spring. Now it's up to you to fill your baskets with spring treasures.

MATERIALS & TOOLS

- 1 roll each Falk Fabric tulle (25 yds) in the following colors:
  - Rosette (basket A)
  - Aqua (basket B)
  - Coral (basket C)
- 1 roll each Falk Fabric netting (40 yds) in the following colors:
  - Paris Pink (basket A)
  - Teal (basket B)
  - Shrimp (basket C)
- Q hook
- Jumbo tapestry needle (such as Clover)
- Thread

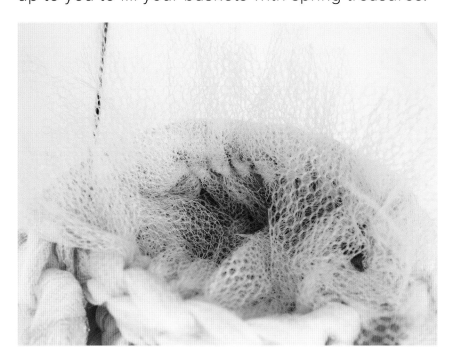

Note: The netting and the tulle are held together throughout the pattern.

Basket A and C Bottom

Ch 3. Join with sl st to form ring.

Rnd 1: Ch 1 (counts as first sc) Sc 5 in the ring. (6 sc)

Mark with a thread the beginning of each rnd. Do not join.

Rnd 2: 2 sc in each sc around. (12 sc)

Rnd 3: *1 sc in next sc, 2 sc in next sc. Repeat from * around. (18 sc)

Basket A and C Sides

Rnd 4: Forming the side of the basket, sc in the back loop only of each sc around. (18 sc)

Rnds 5–6: Sc in each sc around. (18 sc) Do not end. Do not join.

Basket A and C Handle

Sc in next sc. Ch 1 and turn.

Rows 1–12: 1 sc in each of next 2 sc. Ch 1 turn.

Row 13: 1 sc in each of next 2 sc. Turn but do not ch 1.

Join handle to the other side by inserting hook into first sc of the handle and into a sc directly across from the starting position of the handle, YO, and sl st. Insert hook in second sc in handle and into next sc in basket. YO and sl st. Insert hook into next sc in top of the basket. Sl st and end. Weave in tails.

TIP: When weaving tails of wide pieces of fabric, taper the ends. Starting at the cut end of the fabric, working toward the basket, taper the tails. This will make it so much easier to weave in your ends. I recommend you use a Clover jumbo tapestry needle with the bent tip. This needle makes it so easy to work in the tails of the tulle and netting.

Basket B Bottom

Ch 3. Join with sl st to form ring.

Rnd 1: Ch 1 (counts as first sc). Sc 5 in the ring. (6 sc)

Mark with a thread the beginning of each rnd. Do not join.

Rnd 2: 2 sc in each sc around. (12 sc)

Rnd 3: *1 sc in next sc, 2 sc in next sc. Repeat from * around. (18 sc)

Rnd 4: *1 sc in next 2 sc, 2 sc in next sc. Repeat from * around. (24 sc)

Rnd 5: *1 sc in next 3 sc, 2 sc in next sc. Repeat from * around. (30 sc)

Basket B Sides

Rnd 6: Forming the side of the basket, sc in back of loop only of each sc around. (30 sc)

Rnds 7–10: Sc in each sc around. (30 sc) Do not end. Do not join.

Basket B Handle: Sc in next sc. Ch 1 and turn.

Rows 1–17: 1 sc in each of next 2 sc. Ch 1 turn.

Row 18: 1 sc in each of the next 2 sc. Turn but do not ch 1.

See instructions for joining handle from Baskets A and C.

scrappy therapy

I have a confession to make. I tend to be drawn to fiber arts that are fussy and detailed. Every now and then, I have to coax myself away from this natural tendency and do something that is a little out of my control, letting the fiber go where it will. A benefit to this basket is the opportunity to utilize all of those little bits of yarn that you don't know what to do with, but hate to throw away. The more colors and small amounts in different lengths, the better. If you are looking for something that is easy to take in the car, on a plane, or just sitting around in a waiting room, making your scrappy skein is perfect.

YARN

MATERIALS & TOOLS

- 1 skein scrappy yarn
- 1 skein Red Heart Super Saver yarn 312 Black (7 oz/364 yds)
- Size 7 hook
- #18 tapestry or chenille needle
- Stitch markers

> **Note:** You will be holding two strands together throughout the basket.

Make Scrappy Skein

1: You will use a Russian join to join scraps of yarn. Thread one piece of yarn onto the tapestry or chenille needle, leaving as short a tail as possible.

2: Place a second piece of yarn on top of the first piece and under the needle.

3: Sew back into the yarn for about 2 inches, and pull yarn through. Pull tight.

4: Thread the second piece of yarn, leaving as short a tail as possible. Sew back into the yarn for about 2 inches and pull yarn through. Pull tight. You have now completed one join.

5: Continue to join pieces of yarn until you have a large skein. If you run out of scrappy yarn before completing your basket, just add more yarn to the ends.

Bottom

Make a slip knot with your scrappy yarn, ch 4, and join into ring with a sl st.

Rnd 1: 6 sc into ring. Place sm on the last sc—remove each rnd and place on the new last st.

Rnd 2: 2 sc in each sc. (12 sc)

Rnd 3: *Sc 2 in next sc, 1 sc in next sc. Repeat from * across the rnd. (18 sc)

Rnd 4: *Sc 2 in next sc, 1 sc in each of next 2 sc. Repeat from * across the rnd. (24 sc)

Rnd 5: *Sc 2 in next sc, 1 sc in each of next 3 sc. Repeat from * across the rnd. (30 sc)

Rnd 6: *Sc 2 in next sc, 1 sc in each of next 4 sc. Repeat from * across the rnd. (36 sc)

Rnd 7: *Sc 2 in next sc, 1 sc in each of next 5 sc. Repeat from * across the rnd. (42 sc)

Rnd 8: *Sc 2 in next sc, 1 sc in each of next 6 sc. Repeat from * across the rnd. (48 sc)

Rnd 9: *Sc 2 in next sc, 1 sc in each of next 7 sc. Repeat from * across the rnd. (54 sc)

Rnd 10: *Sc 2 in next sc, 1 sc in each of next 8 sc. Repeat from * across the rnd. (60 sc)

Rnd 11: *Sc 2 in next sc, 1 sc in each of next 9 sc. Repeat from * across the rnd. (66 sc)

Rnd 12: *Sc 2 in next sc, 1 sc in each of next 10 sc. Repeat from * across the rnd. (72 sc)

Rnd 13: *Sc 2 in next sc, 1 sc in each of next 11 sc. Repeat from * across the rnd. (78 sc)

Rnd 14: *Sc 2 in next sc, 1 sc in each of next 12 sc. Repeat from * across the rnd. (84 sc)

Rnd 15: *Sc 2 in next sc, 1 sc in each of next 13 sc. Repeat from * across the rnd. (90 sc)

Rnd 16: *Sc 2 in next sc, 1 sc in each of next 14 sc. Repeat from * across the rnd. (96 sc)

Sides

1: Continue crocheting rnds until basket is 4 inches high. Break scrappy yarn and join black yarn.

2: *Sc in each of next 4 sc. Put a sm on 1 of the 2 loops of yarn that is on the hook to hold it in place. Remember that you are using the yarn double. That is why there will be 2 loops on the hook.

3: With the other loop and one of the two strands, ch 13. In the second ch from the hook, sc 2. Continue putting 2 sc in each of the ch stitches. When you reach the top, put the remaining loop back on the hook along with the one that had the sm in it. Pull both strands of yarn tight.* Repeat between the * across the rnd.

4: Sc one more rnd, making sure to go into all of the sc from the previous rnd. Break yarn and work in ends.

feather basket

FINISHED MEASUREMENTS: 17-in. wide by 4-in. high   **GAUGE:** 2 sc = 1½ inches

When I look at this basket, I can almost hear the drums in the background, and picture fields and forests. There was a time when people had to make everything for themselves, by hand. I love that idea! With so much to do just to survive, they took the time to make things beautiful as well as functional. I love that too! This basket is not only functional, but beautiful too, and would make a great addition to any household.

YARN

![5 BULKY]

Materials & Tools

- 1 roll #72 jute twine (4 ply/135 ft)

- P hook

- J hook

- Clear glue (such as Beacon Adhesives' Fabri-Tac)

- 3 ft half-bronze schlappen feathers

Crocheted by Debbie Decker

Bottom

Using the P hook, ch 4. Join to form a ring with a sl st.

Rnd 1: Ch 2 (counts as first dc), 7 dc in ring. Join with sl st to ch 2. (8 dc)

Rnd 2: Ch 2 (counts as first dc), 1 dc in joining st. 2 dc in next dc and in each remaining dc around. Join with sl st to ch 2. (16 dc)

Rnd 3: Ch 2 (counts as first dc), 1 dc in joining st. 2 dc in next dc and in each remaining dc around. Join with sl st to ch 2. (32 dc)

Rnd 4: Ch 2 (counts as first dc), 1 dc in joining st. 2 dc in next dc and in each remaining dc around. Join in back loop of ch 2. (64 dc)

Side

Rnds 5–6: Ch 2 (counts as first dc), 1 dc in back loop of each dc around. Join with sl st in ch 2. (64 dc) End. Weave in tails.

Note: Schlappen feathers are stitched together. Leave the stitching in—it makes it easier to glue them to the finished basket.

Feathers

1: Using clear glue, attach feathers to the bottom inside edge of the basket. The bottom of the feathers should touch the bottom of the basket.

2: To finish the inside of the basket, ch 84 with a J hook. End. Weave in tails. Glue the top of the chain down to cover the stitching on the feathers all the way around the inside of the basket.

key to my heart

This basket solves one eternal problem. What do you do with those keys you are not quite sure what they were for, but are afraid to throw out? In addition to being decorative and functional as a basket, this is a great way to keep those keys handy just in case you remember what they unlocked.

YARN

MATERIALS & TOOLS

- 1 skein Red Heart Super Saver yarn 3901 Rouge (7 oz/364 yds) (color A)
- 1 skein Red Heart Super Saver yarn 0776 Dark Orchid (7 oz/364 yds) (color B)
- G hook
- I hook
- 6 old keys
- 1 yd ⅜-in.-wide red ribbon
- Sewing thread to match the hearts
- Sewing needle
- Pins
- Stitch marker

Note: For the basket, hold two strands together and use the size I hook. For the hearts, use a single strand and size G hook.

Bottom

Make a slip knot with color A, ch 4 and join into ring with a sl st.

Rnd 1: 6 sc into ring. Place sm on the last sc—remove each rnd and place on the new last st.

Rnd 2: 2 sc in each sc. (12 sc)

Rnd 3: *2 sc in next sc, 1 sc in next sc. Repeat from * across the rnd. (18 sc)

Rnd 4: *2 sc in next sc, sc in next 2 sc. Repeat from * across the rnd. (24 sc)

Rnd 5: *2 sc in next sc, sc in next 3 sc. Repeat from * across the rnd. (30 sc)

Rnd 6: *2 sc in next sc, sc in next 4 sc. Repeat from * across the rnd. (36 sc)

Rnd 7: *2 sc in next sc, sc in next 5 sc. Repeat from * across the rnd. (42 sc)

Rnd 8: *2 sc in next sc, sc in next 6 sc. Repeat from * across the rnd. (48 sc)

Rnd 9: *2 sc in next sc, sc in next 7 sc. Repeat from * across the rnd. (54 sc)

Rnd 10: *2 sc in next sc, sc in next 8 sc. Repeat from * across the rnd. (60 sc)

Rnd 11: *2 sc in next sc, sc in next 9 sc. Repeat from * across the rnd. (66 sc)

Rnd 12: *2 sc in next sc, sc in next 10 sc. Repeat from * across the rnd. (72 sc)

Rnd 13: *2 sc in next sc, sc in next 11 sc. Repeat from * across the rnd. (78 sc)

Rnd 14: *2 sc in next sc, sc in next 12 sc. Repeat from * across the rnd. (84 sc)

Rnd 15: *2 sc in next sc, sc in next 13 sc. Repeat from * across the rnd. (90 sc)

Rnd 16: *2 sc in next sc, sc in next 14 sc. Repeat from * across the rnd. (96 sc)

Side

Rnd 1: Sc in back loop across the rnd.

Rnd 2: *Sc across the rnd. Repeat from * until the side measures 4½ inches.

Heart
Make 6.

Make a slip knot with color B, ch 2.

Row 1: 2 sc in second sc from hook, ch 1, turn. (RS)

Row 2: 2 sc in next sc, 1 sc in next sc, ch 1, turn. (WS) (3 sc)

Row 3: 1 sc, 2 sc in next sc, 1 sc. (4 sc)

Row 4: 2 sc in next sc, 1 sc in each of next 3 sc, ch 1, turn. (5 sc)

Row 5: Sc 5, ch 1, turn.

Row 6: 2 sc in next sc, 3 sc, 2 sc in next sc, ch 1, turn. (7 sc)

Row 7: Sc 7, ch 1, turn.

Row 8: 2 sc in next sc, 5 sc, 2 sc in next sc, ch 1, turn. (9 sc)

Row 9: Sc 9, ch 1, turn.

Row 10: 2 sc, 7 sc, 2 sc in next sc, ch 1, turn. (11 sc)

Row 11: Sc 11, ch 1, turn.

Row 12: 2 sc in next sc, 9 sc, 2 sc in next sc, ch 1, turn. (13 sc)

Row 13: Sc 13, ch 1, turn.

Row 14: 2 sc in next sc, 11 sc, 2 sc in next sc, ch 1, turn. (15 sc)

Row 15: Sc 15, ch 1, turn.

Row 16: Sc 7, ch 1, turn.

Row 17: Repeat row 16.

Row 18: Dec 1, 3 sc, dec 1, ch 1, turn. (5 sc)

Row 19: Dec 1, 1 sc, dec 1, ch 1, turn. (3 sc)

Row 20: YO and pull up a loop in all 3 sc. YO and pull through all 4 loops on the hook. YO, break yarn, and pull through remaining loop. Join yarn on the sc left of center sc and repeat rows 16 through 20. Work in ends on the WS of the heart.

Finishing

Cut ribbon into six 5-inch pieces. Insert hook from the RS to the WS just below the center sc between the lobes. Insert hook under one row of crocheting and back to the RS. Hook ribbon and pull halfway through. Tie on key, pulling tight on the ribbon. Repeat on remaining five hearts. Evenly space hearts around the side of the basket and pin in place. Using matching thread, whip-stitch hearts in place.

loopy color block basket

FINISHED MEASUREMENTS: 10-in. wide by 5-in. high   Gauge: 1½ sc = 1 inch

Potholder loops are a delightful material to crochet with. They offer several advantages. With the right hook, a gauge can be achieved that offers enough stiffness for a very sturdy basket. The second reason these cotton loops are so wonderful is that they come in a range of colors, which can be placed where desired within a basket.

YARN

MATERIALS & TOOLS

- 1 10-oz bag each Wool Novelty Company cotton weaving loops in the following colors:
  - Medium blue
  - Dark blue
  - Yellow
  - Medium green
  - Red
- Stitch marker
- Size 19 hook

Note: Join loops as needed.

Make Loopy Yarn

Make 5 yards of blue loopy yarn (medium and dark blue loops mixed) to start with. You will also need lengths of the other individual colors. To make the loopy yarn, take one loop and insert it into another. Insert the end of that loop into itself and pull tight. Two loops are now joined. Insert another loop into one of the joined loops and again insert the end of this loop into itself and pull tight. Repeat as needed.

Bottom

Make a slip knot in the end of the loopy yarn. Ch 2.

Rnd 1: Sc 6 into second ch from the hook.

Rnd 2: Sc 2 in each of 6 sc around. Use sm to mark the last sc made—replace into last st every rnd. (12 sts)

Rnd 3: *Sc 2 in next st, 1 sc in next sc. Repeat from * across the rnd. (18 sts)

Rnd 4: *Sc 2 in next st, 1 sc in each of next 2 sc. Repeat from * across the rnd. (24 sts)

Rnd 5: *Sc 2 in next st, 1 sc in each of next 3 sc. Repeat from * across the rnd. (30 sts)

Rnd 6: *Sc 2 in next st, 1 sc in each of next 4 sc. Repeat from * across the rnd. (36 sts)

Sides

Continue with blue mix for 9 sc. Switch to yellow for 9 sc. Switch to medium green for 9 sc. Switch to red for 9 sc. Repeat between the * for each rnd until the basket measures 5 inches. Pull loopy yarn through last sc worked. Work in ends of unworked loops.

wave your flag

FINISHED MEASUREMENTS: 10-in. wide by 3-in. high   Gauge: 2 st = 1½ inches

This basket should be used all throughout the year—not just on the Fourth of July, or pulling it out in an election year. We should be proud of our country and our flag. Wave your flag all year round. I did not make the sides of this basket too high, so that you can see the red, white, and of course the blue.

MATERIALS & TOOLS

- Blue cotton fabric, 18-in. x 4-ft, washed and dried (color A)
- Off-white cotton fabric, 18-in. x 2-ft, washed and dried (color B)
- Red cotton fabric, 18-in. x 3-ft, washed and dried (color C)
- Q hook
- Scissors or rotary cutter
- Jumbo tapestry needle (such as Clover)

Strips

Cut fabric into 2-inch strips. You will be snipping and ripping (or using a rotary cutter) to transform your cotton fabrics into strips. Join strips as necessary by folding the edge of the strip over about 1 inch. Cut a ½-inch slit into the folded edge of the strip. Repeat with the strip you want to join. Lay the slits on top of each other, with tails facing in opposite directions. Take the tail that is on top and pull it through the bottom of the slits. Pull the two tails in opposite directions. This will tighten the joining knot. Repeat as necessary. I recommend crocheting on top of your tails to cover them.

Basket

Rnd 1: Make a magic ring with color A. 6 sc in ring. Pull tail tight. Do not join. (6 sc) Mark beginning of rounds with thread.

Rnd 2: 2 sc in each sc. Do not join. (12 sc)

Rnd 3: 2 sc in each sc. Do not join. (24 sc)

Rnd 4: *2 sc in next sc, 1 sc in next. Repeat from * around. (36 sc)

Rnd 5: Sc in back loop of each sc. Sl st to first sc. End color A. (36 sc)

Rnd 6: Join color B in sc after sl st of previous round. Ch 2 (counts as hdc). Hdc in next sc, dc in next sc, hdc in next 2 sc, sc in next sc. *Hdc in next 2 sc, dc in next sc, hdc in next 2 sc, sc in next sc.*

Repeat between the * around. Join to top of ch 2 with a sl st. End color B.

Rnd 7: Join color C in next sc after sl st of previous row. Ch 2 (counts as dc). *Sc in dc, dc in next 2 hdc, tr in next sc, dc in next 2 hdc, sc in next dc.* Repeat between the * 5 times. Dc in next 2 hdc, tr in next dc, dc in next hdc. Join with sl st to top of ch 2. End.

If you crocheted on top of your tails, then you can just cut them. If not, taper the tails by cutting from the top of the tail toward the base (closest to the crocheting). This makes it easier to weave in the tails. Use your jumbo tapestry needle to weave in tails.

bathing beauty basket

FINISHED MEASUREMENTS: 7-in. wide by 3-in. high **GAUGE:** 2 sc = ½ inch

I'm always searching in my bathroom closet for things. Do you do that too? I thought it would be a good idea to make a small basket to hold all those items. Each basket holds an item, such as cotton balls, dental floss, cotton swabs, or eyeglass wipes. The size is important on this basket. Most people don't have a lot of room in the bathroom for anything too large. The size is just right for any size bathroom.

YARN

MATERIALS & TOOLS

- 2 skeins lightweight Sari Ribbon by Frabjous Fibers in Sand (25 yds/10–20mm wide)
- J hook
- Safety pins
- Sewing needle
- Sewing thread to match ribbon
- Jumbo tapestry needle
- Stitch marker

Crocheted by Debbie Decker

> **Note:** Mark every rnd with a sm.

Small Baskets

Make 5.

Ch 2.

Rnd 1: Work 6 sc in second ch from the hook.

Rnd 2: Work 2 sc in each of the 6 sc around. (12 sc)

Rnd 3: *Work 2 sc in next sc, then 1 sc in next sc. Repeat from * 1 more time. (18 sc)

Rnd 4: *Work 2 sc in next sc, then 1 sc in each of next 2 sc. Repeat from * 1 more time. (24 sc)

Rnds 5–7: Sc in each sc around. (24 sc)

Rnd 8: Sl st tightly in first sc, ch 1, sc in same sc as sl st. Sc in each remaining sc around, then join with a sl st to the top of the beginning ch 1. End. Weave in tails.

Middle Basket

Make 1.

Ch 2.

Rnd 1: Work 6 sc in second ch from the hook.

Rnd 2: Work 2 sc in each of the 6 sc around. (12 sc)

Rnd 3: *Work 2 sc in next sc, then 1 sc in next sc. Repeat from * 1 more time. (18 sc)

Rnds 4–12: Sc in each sc around. (18 sc)

Rnd 13: Sl st tightly in first sc, ch 1, sc in same sc as sl st. Sc in each remaining sc around, then join with a sl st to the top of the beginning ch 1. End. Weave in tails.

Assembly

1: Pin the baskets together with safety pins, placing the five smaller baskets around the middle basket.

2: Using matching sewing thread that is doubled and knotted at the end, sew the side baskets together first. To do this, hide the knotted end in between the inside stitches. Sew from the inside of one basket, through the top edge, to the inside of the adjoining basket. Go back and forth at least 3 times, through at least 2 of the top edge sc. Knot the end and bury your knot in the crochet stitches.

3: When you have sewn all the little baskets together, then sew the top edge of the small baskets to the middle section of the tall basket in the center. Match the bottom edges of the baskets to make sure you are sewing in the right place on the middle basket.

bridal basket

FINISHED MEASUREMENTS: 11-in. wide by 5½-in. tall   **GAUGE:** 2 sc = 1¼ inch

This idea was inspired by my friend Sharon, who was kind enough to share the story and pattern with me. Her mother made scrubbies, tied here around the outside of the basket, as a fundraiser for her garden club. You got the first one free, but after that you had to purchase them. Load this sturdy basket with your favorite cleaning supplies and soaps as a bridal shower gift. As the new bride cleans her house, she can untie one scrubbie at a time without affecting the basket. When all the scrubbies have been used, she still has a beautiful basket.

YARN

SUPER BULKY

MATERIALS & TOOLS

- 1 skein each Bonnie Braid macrame cord (6mm/100 yds) in the following colors:
  - Almond (color A)
  - Pearl (color B)
  - Brown (color C)
  - Tan (color D)
- 1 roll teal netting, 6-in. x 40-ft., 100% nylon (for scrubbies)
- ⅛ yd dark brown netting, 100% nylon (ties for scrubbies)
- P hook (basket)
- K hook (scrubbies)
- Scissors
- Matches
- Jumbo tapestry needle (such as Clover)
- Stitch markers (such as Clover Wonder Clips)
- Sewing thread to match color A
- Sewing needle

Crocheted by Melissa Polumbus

Bottom

Rnd 1: Starting with color A and a magic ring: 6 sc in ring. Sl st into first sc. (6 sc)

Rnd 2: Ch 1 (counts as first sc), 1 sc in joining. 2 sc in each sc around. Sl st into ch 1. (12 sc)

Rnd 3: Ch 1 (counts as first sc), 2 sc in next sc. *1 sc in next sc, 2 in next sc.* Repeat between the * across the rnd. Sl st in ch 1. End. (18 sc)

Rnd 4: Using color B, join in sl st. Ch 1 (counts as first sc) 1 sc in next sc, 2 in next. *1 sc in next 2 sc, 2 sc in next.* Repeat between the * across the rnd. Sl st in ch 1. (24 sc)

Rnd. 5: Ch 1 (counts as first sc). Sc in next 2 sc, 2 sc in next sc. *1 sc in next 3 sc, 2 sc in next.* Repeat between the * across the rnd. Sl st in ch 1. (30 sc)

Rnd 6: Ch 1 (counts as first sc). Sc in next 3 sc, 2 sc in next sc. *1 sc in first 4 sc, 2 sc in next sc.* Repeat between the * across the rnd. Sl st in ch 1. End. (36 sc)

Rnd 7: Using color C, join to sl st. Ch 1 (counts as first sc). Sc in next 4 sc, 2 sc in next sc. *1 sc in first 5 sc, 2 sc in next.* Repeat between the * across the rnd. Sl st in ch 1. (42 sc)

Rnd 8: *1 sc in first 6 sc, 2 sc in next. Repeat between the * across the rnd. End. (48 sc)

Small Side Circles
Make 7.

Rnd 1: Starting with color C and a magic ring: 6 sc in ring. Sl st into first sc. End. (6 sc)

Rnd 2: Join color D with ch 1 (counts as first sc), 1 sc in joining. 2 sc in each sc around. Sl st into ch 1. End. (12 sc)

Rnd 3: Join color A with ch 1 (counts as first sc), 2 sc in next sc. *1 sc in next sc, 2 in next sc.* Repeat between the * across the rnd. Sl st in ch 1. End. (18 sc)

Lay the bottom of the basket RS up. With the RS of the side circles facing to the outside, pin them to the outside edge of the basket bottom. With matching sewing thread, sew the bottom of the side circles to the outside edge of the bottom. Then sew the sides of the side circles together. If you need to weave tails under the cord, pull tails tight. Clip close to the crocheting. Use a match to burn the end and work it into the crocheting to hide and glue the ends under the crocheting.

Scrubbies
Make 7.

Starting with a 6-inch by 12-foot piece of netting, fold it end to end to make a piece that is 6 inches wide, but only 12 inches long. Then, cut through the folded-up piece to create seven pieces that are 1½ inches by 12 feet. I used Clover Wonder Clips to hold the rest of the netting together until you are ready to cut it. You will use the K hook to crochet the scrubbies.

Put a slip knot in netting every 6 to 10 inches. This will give it extra scrubbing ability.

Rnd 1: Ch 2. 6 sc in second ch from hook. Mark beginning of each rnd with a thread.

Rnd 2: Ch 2. Sc in first sc. *Ch 2. Sc in next sc. Repeat from * across the rnd.

Rnd 3: Ch 2. *Sc in ch 2 space, ch 2. Repeat from * across the rnd.

Rnd 4: Ch 2. *Sc in ch 2 space, ch 2. Repeat from * across the rnd.

Rnd 5: Sc in each sc and 2 sc in each ch 2 space around.

Rnd 6: Sc in back loop of each sc around.

Rnd 7: Sc in each sc around.

Rnd 8: Dec round (back of the scrubby). YO and pull up loop in first sc. YO and pull up loop in second sc. YO and through 3 loops; the dec is made. Repeat around. Keep doing the dec until you reach the center. To end, pull up a loop 1-inch tall. Cut end and pull through loop to form a knot. Pull the knot and tail to the inside of the scrubby.

Cut pieces of the dark brown netting to 7 by 3 inches. Thread onto a jumbo tapestry needle. Insert needle through the front of the scrubbie, just off-center and through the front of the circle to the back of the circle (inside of the basket). Insert needle through the back side of the circle and back side of the scrubbie toward the front. When both ends are in the front of the scrubbie, tie them together just once to hold scrubbie in place. Repeat with remaining scrubbies. Trim the tails of the netting at an angle.

heart basket

FINISHED MEASUREMENTS: 12½-in. wide by 10-in. deep by 3-in. high   **GAUGE:** 2 sc = 1½ inches

Love can fill our hearts with many different reds. It can burn hot with passion and turn it a bright true red. When we lose love, hearts can turn dark and murky, like a burgundy red. Sometimes love will become faded or mellow, like a wine red. Here is a basket that reminds us of all these shades and feelings.

YARN

MATERIALS & TOOLS

- 1 skein each Bonnie Braid macrame cord (6mm/100 yds) in the following colors:
  - Red (Color A)
  - Burgundy (Color B)
  - Wine (Color C)
- P hook
- Matches
- Jumbo tapestry needle (such as Clover)

Crocheted by Melissa Polumbus

Foundation rnd: Using color A, start with a magic ring (does not count as st), working into the ring, work 4 dc, 3 tr, ch 1, sl st in ring, ch 1, and continue working in ring 3 tr, 3 dc, join with a sl st to first dc of round, pull tail of yarn to close up ring. (16 sts)

Rnd 1: Ch 1 (does not count as st), 1 dc in same st as join, 1 dc in each of the next 3 sts, 1 tr in next, 2 tr in next, 3 tr in next, ch 1, sl st in sl st from previous rnd, ch 1, 3 tr in next st, 2 tr in next, 1 tr in next, 1 dc in each of the next 3 sts. Join in ch 1. (22 sts)

Rnd 2: Ch 1 (does not count as st), 1 dc in same st as join, 1 dc in each of the next 5 sts, 1 tr in next, 2 tr in next, 3 tr in next, 2 dc in next, ch 1, sl st in sl st from previous round, ch 1, 2 dc in next, 3 tr in next st, 2 tr in next, 1 tr in next, 1 dc in each of the next 5 sts. Join in ch 1. (30 sts)

Rnd 3: Ch 1 (does not count as st), 1 dc in same st as join. 1 dc in each of the next 6 sts, 2 dc in next, 2 tr in each of the next 3 sts, 3 tr in next, 1 dc in each of the next 2 sts, ch 1, sl st in sl st from previous rnd, ch 1, 1 dc in each of the next 2 sts, 3 tr in next, 2 tr in each of the next 3 sts, 2 dc in next, 1 dc in each of the next 6 sts. Join in ch 1. (42 sts)

Rnd 4: Ch 1 (does not count as st) 1 tr in same st as join, 1 tr in each of the next 19 sts, 1 tr in ch 1 space, skip sl st, 1 tr in ch 1 space, 1 tr in each of the next 19 sts. Join in ch 1. (41 sts)

Rnds 5–7: Using color B, ch 1, tr in each st around, join with sl st in ch 1.

Rnd 8: Using color C, join by inserting hook into back loop of first tr, YO, and sl st. Sl st in the back loops of next 16 tr. Insert hook into next tr back loop and go right through next back loop from back side of loop to the inside of the basket. YO and pull through to sl st through 2 loops. Sl st in back loop of next 20 tr. Skip next tr and insert hook into next back loop of tr and then go back to skipped back loop of previous tr and insert hook. YO and sl st. Sl st in first sl st to end.

Weave in tails. Pull tails tight. Clip close to crocheting. Use a match to burn the end and work it into the crocheting to hide and glue down the ends.

no. 2 pencil

FINISHED MEASUREMENTS: 14½-in. wide by 5-in. high   **GAUGE:** 4 sc = 1 inch

There are so many things in our daily lives that we take for granted, and one of these is the no. 2 pencil. I'm sure many of you, like me, used these while still in school. What opened my eyes to the aesthetics of this writing instrument is an art book I purchased years ago that was filled with images of animals portrayed with drawn no. 2 pencils. My hope with this basket is that you will enjoy a new appreciation for this pencil and for many of the other everyday items we use without studying and appreciating them.

YARN

MEDIUM

MATERIALS & TOOLS

- 1 skein each Berroco Vintage (3½ oz/218 yds) in the following colors:
  - 51180 Grapefruit (color A)
  - 5106 Smoke (color B)
  - 5121 Sunny (color C)
  - 5104 Mushroom (color D)
  - 5145 Cast Iron (color E)
- F hook
- G hook
- Stitch marker

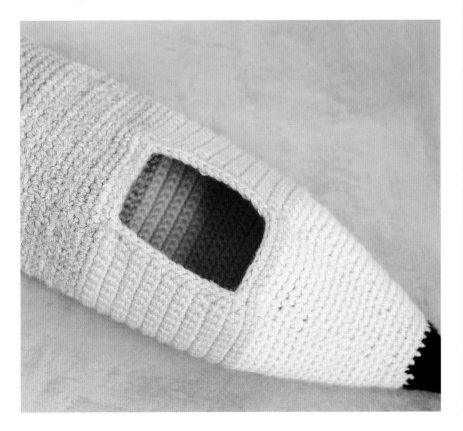

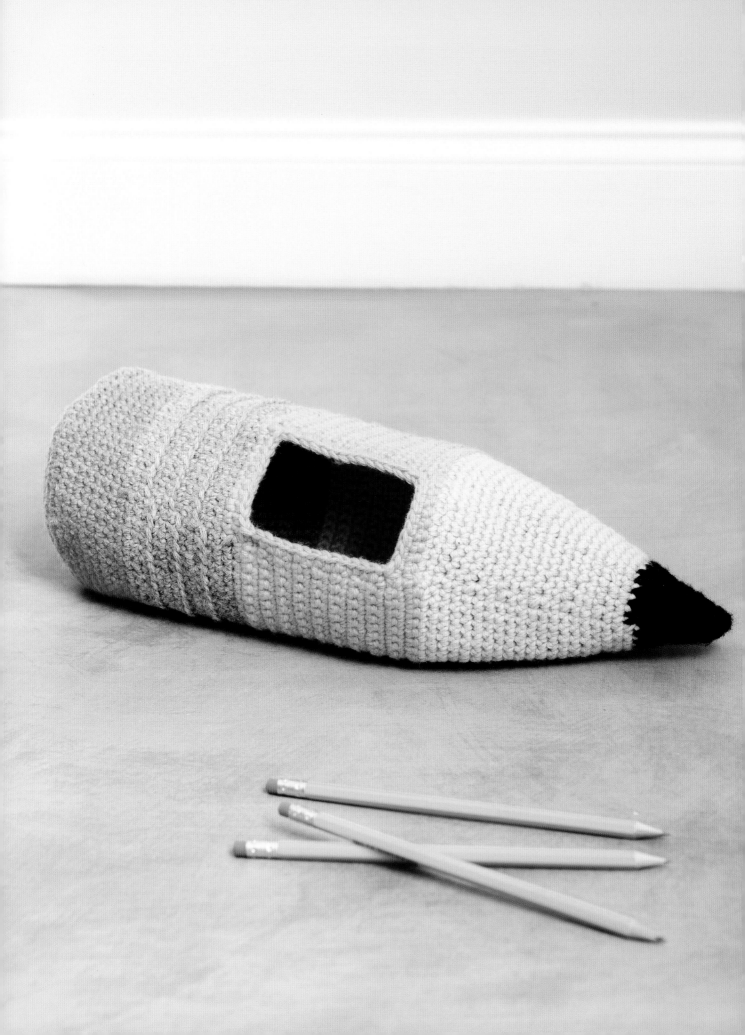

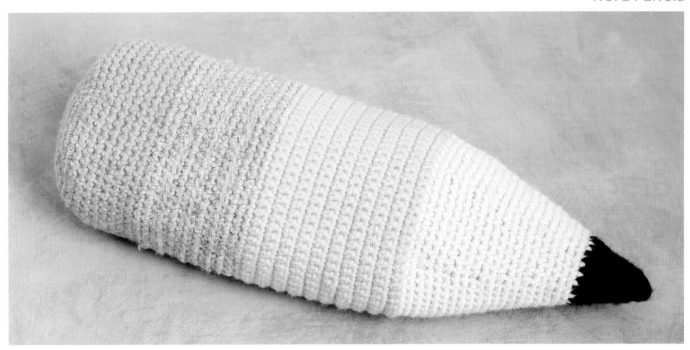

Note: Hold two strands together throughout.

Using color A, make a slip knot with larger hook, ch 4, and join into ring with a sl st.

Rnd 1: 6 sc into ring. Place sm on the last sc—remove each rnd and place on the new last st.

Rnd 2: 2 sc in each sc. (12 sc)

Rnd 3: *Sc 2 in next sc, 1 sc in next sc. Repeat from * across the rnd. (18 sc)

Rnd 4: *Sc 2 in next sc, sc in each of next 2 sc. Repeat from * across the rnd. (24 sc)

Rnd 5: *Sc 2 in next sc, sc in each of next 3 sc. Repeat from * across the rnd. (30 sc)

Rnd 6: *Sc 2 in next sc, sc in each of next 4 sc. Repeat from * across the rnd. (36 sc)

Rnd 7: *Sc 2 in next sc, sc in each of next 5 sc. Repeat from * across the rnd. (42 sc)

Rnd 8: *Sc 2 in next sc, sc in each of next 6 sc. Repeat from * across the rnd. (48 sc)

Rnd 9: *Sc 2 in next sc, sc in each of next 7 sc. Repeat from * across the rnd. (54 sc)

Rnd 10: *Sc 2 in next sc, sc in each of next 8 sc. Repeat from * across the rnd. (60 sc)

Rnds 11–19: Sc 9 rnds without increasing. Break yarn and join color B.

Rnds 20–22: Sc 3 rnds.

Rnd 23: Sc 1 rnd through back loops.

Rnds 24–26: Sc 3 rnds going through both loops.

Rnds 27–34: Rep last 4 rows twice. On the last rnd, go 1 sc past the beginning of the rnd. Break yarn and join color C.

Rnd 35: Sc 1 rnd. Now working in rows.

Rows 36–53: Ch 1, sc in next 50 sts, turn leaving rem sts unworked.

Row 54: Ch 1, sc across the row, ch 10, sl st into the sc on the other edge of the basket opening joining back into the rnd. Now working in rnds.

Rnd 55: Ch 1, turn, and work 60 sc. (WS) Break yarn and join color D.

Rnds 56–57: Sc 2 rnds.

Rnd 58: *Sc 8, dec 1. Repeat from * across the rnd for a total of 6 dec. (54 sc)

Rnds 59–60: Sc 2 rnds.

Rnd 61: *Sc 7, dec 1. Repeat from * across the rnd. (48 sc)

Rnds 62–63: Sc 2 rnds.

Rnd 64: *Sc 6, dec 1. Repeat from * across the rnd. (42 sc)

Rnds 65–66: Sc 2 rnds.

Rnd 67: *Sc 5, dec 1. Repeat from * across the rnd. (36 sc)

Rnds 68–69: Sc 2 rnds.

Rnd 70: *Sc 4, dec 1. Repeat from * across the rnd. (30 sc)

Rnds 70–71: Sc 2 rnds.

Rnd 72: *Sc 3, dec 1. Repeat from * across the rnd. (24 sc) Break yarn and change to color E.

Rnds 73–74: Sc 2 rnds.

Rnd 75: *Sc 2, dec 1. Repeat from * across the rnd. (18 sc)

Rnds 76–77: Sc 2 rnds.

Rnd 78: *Sc 2, dec 1. Repeat from * across the rnd. (12 sc)

Rnd 79-80: Sc 2 rnds.

Rnd 81: *Sc 2, dec 1. Repeat from * across the rnd. (6 sc)

Rnd 82: Sc 1 rnd. Break yarn, pull tight and work in ends.

With color C, sc around basket opening. Pull up a loop in each corner sc, YO, and pull through 3 loops.

polka dot dilemma

FINISHED MEASUREMENTS: 7-in. wide by 4-in. high   **GAUGE:** 3 sc = 1 inch

Have you ever found that perfect something that you had been shopping for, only to be confronted with a choice of which color to choose? I remember once standing at the counter of a little boutique for the longest time, trying to make up my mind whether to get a compact mirror with black background and white dots or a white background and black dots. Silly, I know, and I am not going to tell you which one I chose. The good news with this basket is that you don't have to face that dilemma, because you can crochet one of each color combination.

YARN

MEDIUM

MATERIALS & TOOLS

- 1 skein Red Heart Super Saver Yarn in 0313 Aran (7 oz/364 yds) (color A)
- 1 skein Red Heart Super Saver Yarn in 0312 Black (7 oz/364 yds) (color B)
- I hook
- Stitch marker

> **Note:** Hold two strands together throughout.

Bottom

With color A, make a slip knot. Ch 4 and join into a ring with a sl st.

Rnd 1: 6 sc into ring. Place sm on the last sc. Remove each rnd and place on the new last stitch.

Rnd 2: 2 sc in each sc. (12 sc)

Rnd 3: *2 sc in next sc, 1 sc in next sc. Repeat from * across the rnd. (18 sc)

Rnd 4: *2 sc in next sc, 1 sc in each of next 2 sc. Repeat from * across the rnd. (24 sc)

Rnd 5: *2 sc in next sc, 1 sc in each of next 3 sc. Repeat from * across the rnd. (30 sc)

Rnd 6: *2 sc in next sc, 1 sc in each of next 4 sc. Repeat from * across the rnd. (36 sc)

Rnd 7: *2 sc in next sc, 1 sc in each of next 5 sc. Repeat from * across the rnd. (42 sc)

Rnd 8: *2 sc in next sc, 1 sc in each of next 6 sc. Repeat from * across the rnd. (48 sc)

Rnd 9: *2 sc in next sc, 1 sc in each of next 7 sc. Repeat from * across the rnd. (54 sc)

Rnd 10: *2 sc in next sc, 1 sc in each of next 8 sc. Repeat from * across the rnd. (60 sc)

Sides

Rnds 1–2: Sc across the rnd.

Rnd 3: Start carrying color B by crocheting over it. Between polka dots, pull on color B so that it doesn't show through. Change to the other color by leaving two loops on the hook of the old color. YO with the new color and draw it through the two loops on the hook.

To create polka dots, 3 sc with color A. *With color B, (1 dc, 2tr) all in next st, change back to color A, 5 sc. Repeat from * a total of 9 times. With color B, (1 dc, 2tr) all in next st, change back to color A, 2 sc. That's 10 polka dots made. Break color B.

Rnds 4–5: Sc across the rnd.

Rnd 6: With color B, *(1 dc, 2tr) all in next st. With color A while carrying color B, 5 sc. Repeat from * a total of 10 times. Break color B.

Rnds 7–8: Sc across the rnd.

Rnd 9: Repeat rnd 3.

Rnds 10–11: Sc across the rnd. Break yarn and work in ends.

Make the second basket by reversing the colors.

Roswell

Are you a true believer or a skeptic? The 1947 crash near Roswell, New Mexico continues to stir up controversy to this day. UFO experts assert that an alien space ship crash-landed near the sleepy little town, while the Air Force insists it was nothing more than a weather balloon. No matter which side you take, you will have fun crocheting this glow-in-the-dark basket that is reminiscent of something that might have come from the great beyond.

MATERIALS & TOOLS

- 1 skein each bulky Yummy Yarns Jelly Yarn (200 g/65 yds) in each of the following colors:
  - Vanilla Peppermint Glow (color A)
  - Green Peppermint Glow (color B)
  - Pink Peppermint Glow (color C)
- I metal hook
- Hand lotion
- Stitch marker

> **Note:** It is helpful to rub a little hand lotion on the hook and yarn when crocheting this basket. When joining yarn, make sure to tie with a square knot.

Bottom

Using color A, make a slip knot and ch 2.

Rnd 1: Sc 6 into second ch from hook. Place sm on the last sc in the rnd—replace into last st every rnd.

Rnd 2: Sc 2 in each of 6 sc around. (12 sc)

Rnd 3: *Sc 2 in next sc, 1 sc in next sc. Repeat from * across the rnd. (18 sc)

Rnd 4: *Sc 2 in next sc, 1 sc in each of next 2 sc. Repeat from * across the rnd. (24 sc)

Rnd 5: *Sc 2 in next sc, 1 sc in each of next 3 sc. Repeat from * across the rnd. (30 sc)

Rnd 6: *Sc 2 in next sc, 1 sc in each of next 4 sc. Repeat from * across the rnd. (36 sc)

Rnd 7: *Sc 2 in next sc, 1 sc in each of next 5 sc. Repeat from * across the rnd. (42 sc)

Rnd 8: *Sc 2 in next sc, 1 sc in each of next 6 sc. Repeat from * across the rnd. (48 sc)

Rnd 9: *Sc 2 in next sc, 1 sc in each of next 7 sc. Repeat from * across the rnd. (54 sc)

Rnd 10: *Sc 2 in next sc, 1 sc in each of next 8 sc. Repeat from * across the rnd. (60 sc)

Rnd 11: *Sc 2 in next sc, 1 sc in each of next 9 sc. Repeat from * across the rnd. (66 sc)

Sides

Rnd 1: Continuing with color A, *1 sc in each of next 4 sc, skip next 2 sc, 1 sc in each of next 4 sc, 3 sc into next sc. Repeat from * across the rnd.

Rnd 2: Same as rnd 1. Cut yarn and tie on color B.

Rnds 3–4: Same as rnd 1. Cut yarn and tie on color C.

Rnd 5: Same as rnd 1. Cut yarn and work in ends.

Blocking

If the basket does not sit flat, put it into the dryer for a few minutes. Take out and place on flat surface. While still warm, put weight on the inside of the basket until cooled.

To charge the glow, place under a light or out in direct sunlight.

crown jewels basket

FINISHED MEASUREMENTS: 5-in. wide by 3-in. high   **GAUGE:** 2 puff stitches = 1½ inches

Fit for a queen! This cute little basket is just the perfect size for your treasures. So often, at night especially, it's nice to have a safe place you can put your jewelry. I used two strands of dark variegated yarn to create a dramatic look for the base, and two strands of light and bright variegated yarn to create the "jewels" with a puff stitch.

YARN

MATERIALS & TOOLS

- 1 ball each Noro Kureyon yarn (1¾ oz/110 yds) in the following colors:
  - 310 and 328, held together (color A)
  - 95 and 272, held together (color B)
- J hook
- Jumbo tapestry needle (such as Clover)
- Scissors
- Stitch marker

Rnd 1: Make a magic ring with color A. Ch 1, 6 sc in the ring. Close ring.

Rnd 2: Mark beginning of rnd with thread. 2 sc in each around. (12 sc)

Rnd 3: 2 sc in each sc around. (24 sc)

Rnd 4: 1 sc in each sc around. (24 sc)

Rnd 5: *2 sc in first sc, sc in each next 2 sc. Repeat from * across the rnd. (32 sc)

Rnd 6: * 2 sc in first sc, sc in each of next 3 sc. Repeat from * across the rnd. (40 sc)

Rnd 7: Sc in each sc around. (40 sc)

Rnd 8: Sc in each sc around to last sc. In last sc, hold two loops of sc; drop color A and draw up loop from color B. Do not cut color A.

Rnd 9: Ch 1 and turn. *Sc in first sc. 2 dc in next sc, holding final loop of each dc on the hook. YO and through all three loops at once (the puff stitch has been made). Sc in next sc.* Repeat between the * across the rnd. Drop color B and sl st in first sc with color A.

Rnd 10: Ch 1 with color A and turn. Cut color B. Sc in each sc and puff-stitch across. (40 sc). Join with sl st to ch 1. Do not turn.

Rnds 11–12: Sc in each sc around. Join with sl st to ch 1. Do not turn. (40 sc)

Rnd 13: Pull up loop of color B through loop of color A on hook. Cut color A. Ch 1 and turn. *Sc in first sc. Puff-stitch in next sc, sc in next sc.* Repeat between the * across the rnd. Join with sl st to first sc.

Rnd 14: Pull up loop of color A and pull through color B. Cut color B. Ch 1 and turn with color A. Sc in each sc around. Join with sl st to ch 1. End. Weave in tails with jumbo tapestry needle.

secret saturated sock yarn

FINISHED MEASUREMENTS: 11-in. wide by 4-in. high   **GAUGE:** 1 sc = 1½ inches

It's no secret to anyone who knows me—I love saturated color! When I saw Brown Sheep Company's Wildfoote Luxury Sock Yarn in these bright, beautiful, rainbow colors, I knew I had to create a basket using Rock 'n Roll. Let's face it—most crocheters would not want to make a basket using sock yarn because it would take forever. However, using an automatic spool loom, such as Caron's Embellish-Knit!, a wonderful, thick I-cord yarn can be created to make this basket in a jiffy.

YARN

MATERIALS & TOOLS

- 6 skeins Brown Sheep Company Wildfoote in SY100 Rock 'n Roll (1¾ oz/215 yds)
- N hook
- Stitch marker
- Yarn needle
- Automatic spool loom (such as Embellish-Knit!)

I-Cord

Use an automatic spool loom to make six I-cords—one with each of the skeins of yarn. With a yarn needle, sew the I-cords together to create the yarn for this basket.

Bottom:

Make a slip knot, ch 2.

Rnd 1: 6 sc into the second sc from the hook. Place sm on the last sc. Remove each rnd and place sm on the new last sc.

Rnd 2: 2 sc in each sc. (12 sc)

Rnd 3: *2 sc in next sc, 1 sc in next sc. Repeat from * across the rnd. (18 sc)

Rnd 4: *2 sc in next sc, sc in each of next 2 sc. Repeat from * across the rnd. (24 sc)

Rnd 5: *2 sc in next sc, sc in each of next 3 sc. Repeat from * across the rnd. (30 sc)

Rnd 6: *2 sc in next sc, sc in each of next 4 sc. Repeat from * across the rnd. (36 sc)

Rnd 7: *2 sc in next sc, sc in each of next 5 sc. Repeat from * across the rnd. (42 sc)

Rnd 8: *2 sc in next sc, sc in each of next 6 sc. Repeat from * across the rnd. (48 sc)

Rnd 9: *2 sc in next sc, sc in each of next 7 sc. Repeat from * across the rnd. (54 sc)

Side

Continue crocheting without increasing until yarn runs out. Work in ends.

coloR theoRy nesting baskets

FINISHED MEASUREMENTS: From red to violet: 3¾-in. by 2-in.; 4¼-in. by 2¼; 4¾-in. by 2½-in.; 5¼-in. by 2¾-in.; 5¾-in. by 3-in.; 6¼-in. by 3¼-in. **GAUGE:** 5 sc = 1 inch

I'll just say it. I love color! Mostly pure, saturated color. Somehow the idea of nesting baskets seemed perfect for a very neutral exterior on brightly colored inner baskets. Although these baskets only have the primary and secondary colors, all twelve colors on the color wheel could be crocheted. Just think of the fun in playing with these baskets while experimenting with your own color combinations.

YARN

MATERIALS & TOOLS

- 1 skein each Cascade 220 yarn (3½ oz/220 yds) in the following colors:
  - 8895 Christmas Red (color A)
  - 9542 Blaze (color B)
  - 7828 Neon Yellow (color C)
  - 8894 Christmas Green (color D)
  - 9484 Stratosphere (color E)
  - 9570 Concord Grape (color F)
  - 8555 Black (color G)
  - 2 skeins 9402 Dark Gray & Medium Gray Tweed (color H)
- E hook

Note: The colorful inner basket (colors A through F) will always have one less round than the outer gray basket (color H). The directions will have the round count for the outer basket. Make sure to crochet one less round for the inner basket. Each basket is made of one gray and one colored basket.

Ch 2.

Rnd 1: Sc 6 into second ch from hook.

Rnd 2: Sc 2 in each of 6 sc around. Use sm to mark the last sc made. Replace into last st every rnd. (12 sts)

Rnd 3: *Sc 2 in next st, 1 sc in next sc. Repeat from * across the rnd. (18 sts)

Rnd 4: *Sc 2 in next st, 1 sc in each of next 2 sc. Repeat from * across the rnd. (24 sts)

Rnd 5: *Sc 2 in next st, 1 sc in each of next 3 sc. Repeat from * across the rnd. (30 sts)

Rnd 6: *Sc 2 in next st, 1 sc in each of next 4 sc. Repeat from * across the rnd. (36 sts)

Rnd 7: *Sc 2 in next st, 1 sc in each of next 5 sc. Repeat from * across the rnd. (42 sts)

Rnd 8: *Sc 2 in next st, 1 sc in each of next 6 sc. Repeat from * across the rnd. (48 sts)

Rnd 9: *Sc 2 in next st, 1 sc in each of next 7 sc. Repeat from * across the rnd. (54 sts)

For the red (color A) inner basket, crochet 7 rnds even; for the outer basket (color H), 8 rnds.

For the larger baskets, continue as follows:

Rnd 10: *Sc 2 in next st, 1 sc in each of next 8 sc. Repeat from * across the rnd. (60 sts)

For the orange (color B) inner basket, crochet 8 rnds even; for the outer basket (color H), 9 rnds.

For the larger baskets, continue as follows:

Rnd 11: *Sc 2 in next st, 1 sc in each of next 9 sc. Repeat from * across the rnd. (66 sts)

For the yellow (color C) inner basket, crochet 9 rnds even; for the outer basket (color H), 10 rnds.

For the larger baskets, continue as follows:

Rnd 12: *Sc 2 in next st, 1 sc in each of next 10 sc. Repeat from * across the rnd. (72 sts)

For the green (color D) inner basket, crochet 10 rnds even; for the outer basket (color H), 11 rnds.

For the larger baskets, continue as follows:

Rnd 13: *Sc 2 in next st, 1 sc in each of next 11 sc. Repeat from * across the rnd. (78 sts)

For the blue (color E) inner basket, crochet 11 rnds even; for the outer basket (color H), 12 rnds.

For the largest basket, continue as follows:

Rnd 14: *Sc 2 in next st, 1 sc in each of next 12 sc. Repeat from * across the rnd. (84 sts)

For the violet (color F) inner basket, crochet 12 rnds even; for the outer basket (color H), 13 rnds.

Work in ends on all baskets. Insert inner basket into outer basket, making sure that WS are together. It will be tight and appear that the inner basket is too tall. Line up the beginning/ending of each rnd on the baskets.

Using black (color G), sc both baskets together at the top, starting at the beginning/ending of the baskets. Make sure to go through the loops of both baskets. Break yarn and work in ends.

RESOURCES

ABBREVIATIONS

*Repeat instructions following the asterisk[s] as directed

approx	approximately
beg	begin(ning)
bl	back loop(s)
BPsc	back post single crochet
CC	contrasting color
ch(s)	chain(s) or chain stitch(es)
ch-	refers to chain, or chain space previously made, such as "ch-1 space"
cont	continue(ing)(s)
dc	double crochet(s)
dec(s)	decrease(ing)(s)
fl	front loop(s)
FPsc	front post single crochet
hdc	half double crochet(s)
hdc2tog	half double crochet 2 stitches together— 1 stitch decreased
inc(s)	increase(ing)(s)
lp(s)	loop(s)
MC	main color

mm	millimeter
rep(s)	repeat(s)
rnd(s)	round(s)
RS	right side
sc	single crochet(s)
sc2tog	single crochet 2 stitches together— 1 stitch decreased
sk	skip
sl	slip
sl st(s)	slip stitch(es)
sm	stitch marker
sp(s)	space(s)
st(s)	stitch(es)
tog	together
tr	treble crochet
WS	wrong side
YO(s)	yarn over(s)
yd(s)	yard(s)

CROCHET HOOK SIZES

Millimeter	U.S. Size*
2.25 mm	B-1
2.75 mm	C-2
3.25 mm	D-3
3.5 mm	E-4
3.75 mm	F-5
4 mm	G-6
4.5 mm	7
5 mm	H-8
5.5 mm	I-9
6 mm	J-10
6.5 mm	K-10½
8 mm	L-11
9 mm	M/N-13

*Letter or number may vary. Rely on the millimeter sizing.

METRIC CONVERSIONS

In this book, we've used inches, yards, and ounces, showing anything less than one as a fraction. If you want to convert those to metric measurements, please use the following formulas:

Fractions to Decimals

⅛ = .125
¼ = .25
½ = .5
⅝ = .625
¾ = .75

Imperial to Metric Conversion

LENGTH

Multiply inches by 25.4 to get millimeters
Multiply inches by 2.54 to get centimeters
Multiply yards by .9144 to get meters

For example, if you wanted to convert 1⅛ inches to millimeters:
- 1.125 in. x 25.4 mm = 28.575 mm

And to convert 2½ yards to meters:
- 2.5 yd. x .9144 m = 2.286 m

WEIGHT

Multiply ounces by 28.35 to get grams

For example, if you wanted to convert 5 ounces to grams:
- 5 oz. x 28.35 g = 141.75 g

RESOURCES

SUPPLIERS

Bee Line Art Tools
866-218-1590
www.beelinearttools.com

Bernoulli Brew Werks
www.bernoullibrews.com

Berroco, Inc.
401-769-1212
www.berroco.com

Brown Sheep Company, Inc.
www.brownsheep.com

Cascade Yarn
www.cascadeyarns.com

Clover Needlecraft, Inc.
800-233-1703
www.clover-usa.com

Coats and Clark
www.makeitcoats.com

**Denise Interchangeable
Knitting and Crochet**
www.knitdenise.com

Dewberry Ridge
636-583-8112
www.dewberryridge.com

Dorr Mill Store
800-846-3677
www.dorrmillstore.com

Falk Fabrics LLC
518-725-2777
FJE545@aol.com

Frabjous Fibers
802-257-4178
www.shop.frabjousfibers.com

Lacis
510-843-7178
www.lacis.com

Let Nola Do It, LLC
www.nolahooks.com

Lion Brand Yarns
www.lionbrand.com

Lolo and Eddie
305-724-3799

Minick and Simpson
www.minickandsimpson.
blogspot.com

ParaWire
973-672-0500
www.parawire.com

PattieWack Designs
www.pattiewack.com

Pepperell Braiding Company
800-343-8114
pepperell.com

Skif International
314-773-4401
www.skifo.com

Tulle Source
877-885-5348
www.tullesource.com

Wool Novelty Company
800-831-1135
www.weavingloops.com

> While specified brands of yarn were used in the making of the baskets in this book,
> feel free to use your favorite brand of yarn. (Available online and through your local yarn shop.)

YARN WEIGHT CHART

Yarn Weight Symbol & Category Names	0 LACE	1 SUPER FINE	2 FINE	3 LIGHT	4 MEDIUM	5 BULKY	6 SUPER BULKY	7 JUMBO
Types of Yarns in Category	Fingering, 10 count crochet thread	Sock, Fingering, Baby	Sport, Baby	DK, Light Worsted	Worsted, Afghan, Aran	Chucky, Craft, Rug	Bulky, Roving	Jumbo, Roving

Source: Craft Yarn Council's www.YarnStandards.com

ABOUT THE AUTHORS

Nola A. Heidbreder has been teaching fiber art and handwork for 20 years from her studio in St. Louis, Missouri, and across the country. She has written articles and projects for *Mary Engelbreit's Home Companion* and *Rug Hooking Magazine,* as well as co-authoring several books, and has appeared on local and national television news programs.

Linda Pietz learned to knit at the age of four and has spent more than 40 years passing on her love of knitting and other crafts through classes and workshops. She designs patterns for Bucilla, Dimensions, Cat's Cradle, and other companies, has been featured in several books, has co-authored books with Nola, and has written articles for *Rug Hooking Magazine* and other national magazines. She lives in northern California.

Nola and Linda have collaborated in the past to create *Knitting Rugs: 39 Traditional, Contemporary, Innovative Designs* and *Crocheting Rugs: 40 Traditional, Contemporary, Innovative Designs.*

INDEX

Note: *Italic* text indicates projects

1970s Shag, 47

A
A Penny for Your Thoughts, 23
abbreviations, 125
adjustable ring, 11
automatic spool loom, 121

B
back post stitches, 8
Basket Weave Basket, 69
basket weave texture, 71
Bathing Beauty Basket, 97
beads, 31
Bird's Nest, 63
Blushing Beaded Alligator, 29
bobble clusters, 13
Bottle Cap Basket, 35
bottle caps, 35
Bridal Basket, 101

C
chain space, 10
chain stitch, 6
changing colors, 11
clusters, 12
Color Theory Nesting Baskets, 123
cotton weaving loops, 62, 93
crochet hook sizes, 125
cross stitch, 65
Crown Jewels Basket, 117
cushion, making a, 62

D
decreasing clusters, 13
double crochet, 7
"Dyed" Plarn, 17

E
Easter Parade, 75
elastic band, attaching, 52

F
fabric, crocheting with, 22, 44, 52, 96
Feather Basket, 85
feathers, attaching, 87
felting, 40, 68
filet crochet, 40
Flag Basket, 21
Flower Garden, 67
flowers, crocheting, 68, 77
front post stitches, 8

G
glow-in-the-dark yarn, 113
guitar pick punch, 15

H
half double crochet, 7
Heart Basket, 105
hearts, crocheting, 90
hook sizes, 125
Hook, Yarn, Crochet, 57
Hundertwasser's Spiral, 53

I
I-cord, making, 121
invisible fasten off, 12

K
Key to My Heart, 89
keys, 89
knots in yarn, 12

L
Loopy Color Block Basket, 91
Loopy Pet Bed, 61
loopy yarn, making, 62, 93

M
mattress stitch, 13
metric conversions, 125

N
nesting baskets, 123
No. 2 Pencil, 107

P
pet bed, 61
Picture This, 51
plarn, 17
plastic yarn, 17
Polka Dot Dilemma, 111
post stitches, 8
puff stitch, 12
Put a Lid on It!, 73
right side, 11
Rock 'n' Roll, 15
Roswell, 113

R
round, working in, 10
rows, working in, 10

S
scrappy skein, making, 84
Scrappy Therapy, 83
scrubbies, making, 102
Secret Saturated Sock Yarn, 119

shisa embroidery, 23, 25
single crochet decreases, 8
single crochet, 7
skipping stitches, 8
slip stitch, 6
slipknot, 6
Spring Trio, 79
starting chain, working into both sides, 11
stitches, where to work, 9
stitches
    back post stitches, 8
    bobble clusters, 13
    chain space, 10
    chain stitch, 6
    decreasing clusters, 13
    double crochet, 7
    front post stitches, 8
    half double crochet, 7
    invisible fasten off, 12
    mattress stitch, 13
    post stitches, 8
    puff stitch, 12
    single crochet decreases, 8
    single crochet, 7
    skipping stitches, 8
    slip stitch, 6
    slipknot, 6
    treble crochet, 7
    whip stitch, 13
    yarn over, 6
Sunflower and Daisy Variation, 33
suppliers, 126

T
Tiny Wire Basket, 45
Topsy-Turvy Tool Tote Basket, 43
treble crochet, 7
Tulip Time, 39
tulle, 79

W
Wave Your Flag, 95
weaving strips, 28
whip stitch, 13
wire, crocheting with, 46
Woven, 27
wrong side, 11

Y
yarn over, 6
yarn weight chart, 126

MORE GREAT BOOKS *from*
SPRING HOUSE PRESS

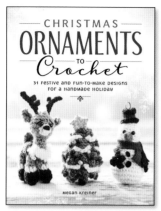

Christmas Ornaments to Crochet
978-1-940611-48-8
$22.95 | 136 Pages

Construction Vehicles to Crochet
978-1-940611-57-0
$22.95 | 120 Pages

Emoji Crochet
978-1-940611-72-3
$16.99 | 80 Pages

Weighted Blankets, Vests & Scarves
978-1-940611-46-4
$12.99 | 48 Pages

Fabulous Fat Quarter Aprons
978-1-940611-39-6
$12.99 | 56 Pages

The Natural Beauty Solution
978-1-940611-18-1
$19.95 | 128 Pages

SPRING HOUSE PRESS